# Sussex Characters
### Wacky, Weird and Wonderful

## Bowen Pearse

By the same author
*Companion to Japanese Britain & Ireland*
*Kent Women*


## To Janice, my best critic

First published in 2001
© 2001 Bowen Pearse
The moral right of the author has been asserted

Published by JAK and distributed by S.B. Publications
19 Grove Road, Seaford, East Sussex BN25 1TP
Tel: 01323 893498   Fax: 01323 893860
Email: sales@sbpublications.swinternet.co.uk
www.sbpublications.swinternet.co.uk

*Front Cover illustrations* - clockwise from top left
The Great Omi, Dolly Shepherd, Archie Belaney, Grey Owl

*Back Cover illustration* - The Piltdown Men (see p54)

ISBN 9523491 4 0

Designed by EH Graphics (01273) 515527

# CONTENTS

# FOREWORD

For a thousand years and more, the county of Sussex has produced millions of stories about men and women who have inhabited its green landscape. This book is about sixteen of them who, for one reason or another, have made themselves memorable and quotable. The lives they lived and the exploits they carried out, enabled them to stand out from their peers.

These sixteen are a varied lot, each with his or her own particular contribution to the county. Some are national or international figures, others are hardly known within the Sussex borders. But they deserve to be remembered for the indelible mark they have left upon their county. Some characters were born in Sussex, some died in Sussex, others made their rare contribution to the world or carried out their crimes on Sussex soil.

There are the middle class 'officer and gentleman' who turned himself into a circus freak; the murderer who drank his victims' blood; the family of singers who have preserved their traditional songs of old Sussex and recited them to listeners all over the world. There is also the strange tale of the Hastings lad who fooled the world into thinking he was a Red Indian, as native Americans were once called, and drew thousands upon thousands to listen to his message of peace and conservation. Still other characters invented things that changed the world. Seldom if ever has such an eclectic group of people come together in one Sussex book.

*Bowen Pearse*

# ACKNOWLEDGEMENTS

So many people have helped put this book together that I hope those I have missed will forgive the omission. I want particularly to thank the librarians of Sussex and Kent who have managed to find me obscure titles, cuttings and archive material, which have helped put skin and bones on little known Sussex characters. My special thanks goes to Sharon Searle for her list of suggestions, and to Barry Russell for winkling out details of the Great Omi and Count Stenbock. I am also indebted to Molly Sedgwick for information and photographs of her mother, Dolly Shepherd. And thanks also to my wife for her painstaking reading of the manuscript. To anybody I have missed, many apologies...

# The Immaculate Crook

## HORATIO WILLIAM BOTTOMLEY (1860-1933)

Horatio Bottomley, whose lavish mansion was at Upper Dicker, has been called the world's greatest swindler. He was also the founder of tabloid journalism, a skilled journalist, a Member of Parliament, a popular country squire, a gifted amateur lawyer and a charismatic orator. He was even tipped to be a future Prime Minister, and dubbed the 'Napoleon of Finance'. But at the end of it all, he was also a convicted criminal.

This extraordinary character was born to a poor family in Hackney, in London's East End, on March 23, 1860. His 'official' parents were Elizabeth and William Bottomley, but there has always been speculation as to whether his real father was the famous Victorian atheist, Charles Bradlaugh. We shall never know for sure as Bradlaugh's papers were heavily censored by his daughter.

It is, however, interesting to consider several factors. Elizabeth was a beautiful woman who had probably accepted William Bottomley for a husband as she was desperately poor and he was the best thing to have come her way. William, however, had suffered from spells of madness and it is likely that Elizabeth refused to have intercourse with him after this discovery, for fear of having insane children.

It is also known that Elizabeth worshipped Bradlaugh, a near neighbour to where they lived in Bethnal Green. Bradlaugh's own marriage was probably a loveless one as his wife had become a dipsomaniac. Thus there were two unhappy families at a time when the law did not permit divorce on the grounds of madness or alcoholism. With this background, many believed that Elizabeth and Bradlaugh became lovers. In some people's minds, even stronger evidence of parenthood is shown by the fact that Horatio bore a striking resemblance to Bradlaugh.

Whatever was the case, William died insane at an early age and Elizabeth died before Horatio was five years old.

His uncle, GJ Holyoake, had the young Horatio placed in the St Josiah Mason Orphanage at Erdington in Birmingham. At the age

*Horatio Bottomley MP arriving at the House of Commons for the debate on the Home Rule Bill, April 11, 1912*

of fourteen he ran away and became an errand boy for a couple of years. His next job was in the office of a solicitor's clerk. Here he began to learn something of the financial world. However, after seeing the chief clerk arrested for fraud, Horatio decided to look for another job.

About this time, his Uncle George Jacob, thinking that a course of shorthand would improve Horatio's prospects, sent him to Pitman's College, where he showed great aptitude. In his spare time Horatio worked in his uncle's publishing enterprise. For ever afterwards Horatio was drawn like a magnet to printer's ink and all that it stood for. He began to do odd jobs for Charles Bradlaugh's *National Reformer,* and met Bradlaugh for the first time.

Bradlaugh recognised Horatio's natural talent and introduced him to the world of books and culture.

From this time onwards Bradlaugh had a great influence on Horatio's future. Bottomley wrote later: 'I soon became captivated by the magnetic personality of Charles Bradlaugh, who became my political and spiritual mentor.'

Horatio became a

shorthand writer for a firm of solicitors in the Supreme Court. His miserly salary was supplemented by Bradlaugh, who continued to help and educate the promising lad. Years later, he described this period as the time he spent in the University of Life.

In 1880, when he was living in Battersea, Bottomley had met and married a local girl, Eliza, daughter of Samuel Norton, a debt collector. She worked in a dressmaker's shop, was far below her husband in intelligence and played only a small part in his life, benefiting little from his success. They had one daughter, Florence. The Bottomleys first made their home in the City but later moved to Clapham. Here he was venerated as 'a pillar of the Methodist Church', while in reality he was a virulent atheist.

At the age of only twenty-four, he set himself up as a publisher. He bought a small ailing newspaper, the *Hackney Hansard,* and a couple of small printing firms. The business flourished and he started further publications. In 1889, he floated the Hansard Publishing Union with a capital of £500,000. But Bottomley had over-reached himself. In 1891 his financial interests crashed, leaving him bankrupt and facing a charge of conspiracy to defraud.

Extreme adversity seemed to bring out the best in Bottomley, allowing him to shine in an entirely new way. He faced the charges with a brilliance of wit and oratory and a deep knowledge of the legal system. He spent his time in court correcting the judge on points of law, tying the prosecution up in knots, and convincing jury, public and judge that he was a victimised underdog. The judge, Mr Justice Hawkins, was so impressed with his performance that he strongly urged him to take up law as a profession.

There is evidence that Bottomley took this advice to heart but, failing to gain admission to any Inn of Court, he instead flung himself into the business of high finance. He founded the Joint Stock Trust and Institute and floated a number of Australian gold-mining companies (one appropriately named Nil Desperandum Mines). Few of his companies paid shareholders and this allowed Bottomley to amass a fortune. His total capital, extending over more than fifty companies, amounted to more than £20,000,000, a staggering amount around the turn of the nineteenth century. In 1897 he featured in the *Financial Times'* series 'Men of Millions'.

Bottomley bought *The Sun* newspaper in 1898 and founded *John Bull* in 1906 with an expenditure of more than £96,000. He was asked to write for the *Sunday Pictorial* for £100 an article – an unheard-of-sum in those days – so he commissioned others to write the articles for him and paid them a quarter of the fee. Later, he even had the £100 fee increased. However, he sacrificed this privileged position to found the *Sunday Illustrated* – which failed.

Substantial sums of money continued to come in; as much went out. Bottomley started a racing stable in 1898 and won several significant prizes. But he made little effort to understand horses or the racing game itself and squandered large sums on racing and gambling, theatrical adventures, and lawsuits. He had a luxurious flat in Pall Mall and a villa in France. There was lavish expenditure on travel, entertainment, gifts and on his so-called 'harem' of mistresses.

A few years earlier he had acquired a country cottage in Upper Dicker, near Hailsham in Sussex. He called the house The Dicker and began to enlarge it, year by year, until – in the words of one observer – it became 'a vast, rambling, hideously ugly mansion where half-a-dozen, then twenty or thirty weekend guests might be accommodated'.

Adjacent land was bought befitting a country estate and a field was converted into an ornamental lake with its own well and pumping station. Eight gardeners tended the grounds and tennis court, and a large staff was also employed in the house. In fact, everything was in place to allow Bottomley to play the position of a real country squire. The Dicker had the only telephone in the village and the squire allowed locals to use it.

Bottomley had his racehorses trained a few miles away at Alfriston. Doing nothing by halves, he often bet £250 each way on his own horses, and when he attended race meetings he gambled away hundreds of thousands of pounds.

Today, The Dicker contains the dinning room, offices and the girls' boarding house of St Bede's School.

One of Bottomley's greatest ambitions was to become a Member of Parliament. At his third attempt, following two near-misses, he won the Liberal seat in South Hackney in the 1906 general election. He had been an enthusiastic and imaginative campaigner, issuing humorous pamphlets and parading his race horses, each with a notice on its saddlecloth, 'Vote for My Owner'.

But despite Bottomley's apparent success in so many fields, there were a number of people who began seriously to question his financial methods. In 1907 the shareholders of the Joint Stock Trust and Institute petitioned for its liquidation. Bottomley's books – the most important of which were unavailable – were examined over a period of eighteen months. He was charged with fraud at the Guildhall in 1909 but once again his skill and wit at court not only drew the crowds, it also got him acquitted.

Then came the case in which a Mrs Curtis sued him for the £50,000 he had obtained from her aged father. This time he lost. In fact, for a while, it seemed his usual luck had left him. By 1911 his financial position was so desperate that he was forced to present a petition in bankruptcy, disclosing liabilities of £233,000 and £50,000 assets. Shrewdly, he had placed both The Dicker and his French villa in his wife's name, so these could not be seized. In 1912, he applied for the Chiltern Hundreds (a device allowing an MP to resign, which he may not do directly).

The outbreak of the First World War brought new opportunities. He vowed to break with his 'sordid past' and became the nation's so-called 'recruiting sergeant'. His many jingoistic speeches brought him at least £50 each. His patriotic ranting, avidly read in the *Sunday Pictorial* and *John Bull,* made him a national figure. He regained his seat at South Hackney, this time as an Independent, with a massive majority.

Stimulated by his popularity, he again began to set up financial operations that – this time – were to bring about his ruin. In 1919 he organised the infamous Victory Bond fraud. He received subscriptions of nearly £900,000. This enabled him to pay off his creditors and he was relieved from his bankruptcy.

But suspicions were already beginning to be felt and demands for repayment began to pour in. Bottomley blustered that if any move were made to prosecute him, 50,000 ex-servicemen would march on Westminster. However, he also admitted privately to a friend: 'I have been sitting on a keg of gunpowder for years and it might go up at any moment'.

Chancery appointed a receiver to examine his financial dealings and in March 1922 he was charged at Bow Street with fraudulent conversion and was committed for trial. The trial was headline news but Bottomley was so confident that once again he would defeat the prosecution, he bought tickets for the forthcoming Epsom race meeting. But the swindler's luck had finally run out. He was found

*Bottomley, centre, arrives at Bow Street, October 1922. On the left is his associate*
*Arthur Newton, on the right his valet Rawson.*

guilty on twenty-three of twenty-four counts and sentenced to seven years in prison.

At Wormwood Scrubs, the prison officials couldn't find a uniform large enough to fit the short, seventeen-stone convict. After years of the good life, Bottomley found prison conditions particularly hard. While he was sewing mailbags, a visitor is said to have recognised the erstwhile financier and said to him: 'Sewing, I see.'

'No, reaping', was the reply.

The prison sentence had stunned his adopted county, Sussex, and nowhere more so than at Upper Dicker. Just prior to his release in 1927, a *Daily Sketch* reporter was sent to Bottomley's home village to see how the locals were reacting to the impending release of their squire. 'Bottomley is Dicker and Dicker without Bottomley is a sad place,' said Mrs Prevett, the stationmaster's daughter. 'Dicker has gone to pieces since Bottomley went away.' Many remembered the red cottages the squire had built for the work people and which he let to them at such reasonable rents. There was talk of decking out the village with banners, and engaging the Hailsham Prize Band to welcome him home.

But not everyone felt the same. Many friends and associates now cut him dead. Bottomley, a great name dropper, told a doctor friend who was on his way to see a patient, Sir Douglas Hogg, at Hailsham, 'give my love to Douglas'. When the message was passed on, Sir Douglas (later to become Lord Hailsham) reacted with fury. 'How dare that scoundrel send me a message?' he demanded.

It was a sad end to a colourful life. Somehow, Bottomley seemed to have lost his spark. He launched *John Blunt,* a successor to *John Bull,* and it failed. He began and finished a world speaking tour in South Africa. Pathetically, he even appeared at the Windmill. But like the listeners on his speaking tour, audiences were no longer interested in an old man reciting anecdotes about the Great War. And when his wife died on February 7, 1930, he felt it badly. The failure of *John Blunt* and his other projects forced him to go bankrupt for the fourth time and he even lost his beloved house at Lower Dicker.

It was reported in April 1933 that he had applied for an old-age pension in recognition of his war services. It had been humiliating to ask for it, and was a very bitter blow when he was turned down.

In May 1933 he collapsed and was taken to the Middlesex Hospital, suffering from cerebral thrombosis caused by arteriosclerosis. He survived an operation but this was followed by a sudden stroke and he died at eleven that night. According to his wishes, his ashes were scattered on the gallops of the South Downs.

# So the Old Songs Need Never Die
## Bob Copper (1915-)

The old Sussex songs are alive and well in the hands of Bob Copper and his family. Bob is in his eighties, has a sweet singing voice, a grey beard and eyes that dance with merriment. He is the senior voice in the family of singing Coppers whose members have worked and sung in Sussex for seven generations with their own style of traditional English folk music.

Under Bob's lead, the Coppers sing unaccompanied songs passed down the centuries, or picked up from contemporaries. They sing in pubs with a couple of pints inside them, at harvest suppers, at ploughing matches, at sheep-shearing feasts and other gatherings. And they sing about the things that have always been put to music – the joys of country life, love, death and war. Some are cradle songs, some comic ditties.

Bob left school at thirteen, though you'd never guess it. The author of six widely-acclaimed books, he talks easily of the hard life on the farm before the war, of the family's singing success at the Albert Hall or about their latest tour of the United States. After ten minutes with Bob you'll know he's well educated in everything that matters. And perhaps to underline this, he has recently been awarded an honorary MA by the University of Sussex.

The tradition of homespun, unaccompanied singing can be traced back to George Copper, born in 1784, when the family name was already two centuries old. The Coppers trace their lineage in a direct line to the late sixteenth century. Rottingdean parish records show Copper baptisms, marriages and burials from 1593.

Bob's grandfather, James, known locally as Brasser, was born in 1845. He was the son of a farm carter or waggoner. The family lived in one of the two-up-two-down flint cottages in Rottingdean, just off the High Street and a stone's throw from the sea. James' working life was spent on the farm and times weren't always easy. He endured hard, heavy work and 'the endless struggle to maintain a decent level of honesty and respectability every day', but rose to become the farm bailiff.

Brasser's son, and Bob's father, was Jim Copper, who also worked his way up to be the bailiff on the 3,000-acre Challoners Farm at Rottingdean. It was an important position, heading a work force of around sixty. Jim was responsible for the buying and selling of stock and generally running the farm. Then, in 1928, when Jim was forty-six, the farmland was sold for housing and he lost his job. Those were the depression years and jobs were hard to come by. 'It was a big come-down,' Bob remembers. Eventually his father found a job as a labourer. The Coppers kept their tied cottage but, previously free, the rent was now eight shillings a week, an extra hardship for, as Bob says, ' eight bob was eight bob', quite a lot of money in those days.

Bob's first job at thirteen was as a tar-boy. This involved treating, with powdered lime, the small cuts on sheep made by the shearers' shears. Before Bob's time tar was used, hence the name. His first full-time job was as a lather-boy in the village barber's shop.

None of these early jobs suited him and he even thought of joining the French Foreign Legion. Instead, he became a cavalry man in the Lifeguards, but soon realised that this too was a bad mistake. He persuaded his parents to buy him out of the army for the then princely sum of £35. He joined the police, where the pay was greater and conditions better. He stayed in the force for ten years – long enough to get used to the inevitable teasing of a Copper being a copper.

This was followed by two years running a Hampshire inn before Bob took over the Central Social Club in Peacehaven with his son John. Here the past lives on in sheep bells over the bar, tables made out of old wagons and wooden models of farm implements. It is a reminder of life on a Sussex farm where Bob's father, Jim, and his grandfather, James, worked.

Bob still lives in the Peacehaven bungalow, with an acre of garden, he's had for more than half a century, and his son and daughter are nearby. Countryside once came to the door; now buses have replaced the horses that used to canter past.

Through the generations the Coppers have never turned professional and for a very good reason. As a BBC man pointed out to Bob: 'Use a musical accompaniment, and there are thousands better than you. Sing as you sing now, and you're unique.'

When Bob and Jim first broadcast from the Eight Bells in

Jevington, in the BBC's *Country Magazine* programme in 1950, it marked the beginning of a revival of English folk singing. Bob still has the yellowing copy of the *Radio Times* with his father's picture on the cover.

'The individuality of the Coppers' style of harmonising is something of an aural illusion,' wrote Al Lloyd in the *Journal of the English Folk Dance & Song Society* in 1952. 'The strangeness, if any, lies in those details which elude normal musical notation – the tone of voice, the slides, scoops and hovers by which the passage from one note to another is affected, the almost imperceptible tremble by which many English folk singers often imply, rather than prove an ornament . . . The Coppers' versions differ only from conventional settings by being rougher, more rudimentary . . . it probably represents a survival of a practice once much more widespread in rural England.'

Listen with your heart as well as your ears and you realise that what you're hearing has existed, unchanged, for more than two centuries. With the help of several LPs and CDs the audience for Copper family songs has spread across the nation and overseas. The Coppers were just in time to preserve an old tradition before it, too, disappeared with the horse-drawn plough and pitch-forked haymaking.

In 1952 four members of the family (Jim and Bob, Jim's brother John, and his son Ron) drew rapturous applause when they sang at the English Folk Dance and Song Society's festival at the Royal Albert Hall. According to the music critic of *The Star:* 'They came on in their work-a-day clothes, spurning a microphone and sang naturally and sweetly'. Now, half a century on, the Coppers are still as active as they've ever been, continuing a family tradition that must be rare in Western music.

When, in 1971, Bob's first book, *A Song for Every Season,* was published, the world seemed to be clamouring for just such a book. Not only did it sell well in America as well as Britain, it was awarded the Beaverbrook Press Robert Pitman £1,000 Literary Award for the Best First Book of the Year.

Although he calls it hard work, writing seems to come easily to Bob. It's a talent that he's always possessed. He explains: 'It was the material I had to work on. It was just a matter of rewriting and getting it down.'

The material came from his father's notebooks, written in clear, neat copperplate handwriting, completed shortly before Jim died. They give a unique account of life lived by ordinary folk on a Sussex farm during the early days of the nineteenth century. The story starts with Bob's grandfather, who headed a team of some sixty men; they sang as they worked in the fields, and they sang, too, at village gatherings.

There are recollections of ploughing with oxen, of the sheep-shearers working for eighteen shillings a week, of the excitement at the arrival of the steam-driven threshing machine and of the various festivals celebrated by the farm hands – and the songs that went with each occasion in the farming calendar.

Even in Brasser's time there was concern that some of the old songs would be lost if they were not set down, and the daughter of the farmer for whom he worked persuaded Brasser to write down as many as he could remember.

In 1898 a similar request was made by a Mrs Kate Lee, a visitor to Rottingdean from London. Brasser and his younger brother, Tom, were invited to sing their full repertoire. A bottle of whisky was put on the table in front of the brothers – 'and you won't leave till you've finished everything and the bottle is empty,' the enthusiastic Mrs Lee told them.

Then, once they were in the mood, they sang until they could remember no more. Mrs Lee wrote down the words and music of 'about half a hundred' songs and it was largely as a result of her interest that the Folk Song Society (later the English Folk Dance & Song Society – EFDSS) was formed in 1899. Brasser and Tom were made honorary founder members.

It seemed that everything had to be celebrated with a song. The end of potato planting was marked by the *Tater Beer Night*. There was the *Black Ram* at sheep-shearing time, and *Hollerin' Pot* at the conclusion of the harvest.

In the early 1920s the wireless appeared in more and more homes, with music from America and other parts of the world. But there were still families who would keep the old songs alive, and Bob's family was one of these.

Bob's writing is warm with nostalgia. He paints a picture of the Copper family sitting around the kitchen range, his mother on one side darning socks and his father on the other making rabbit nets.

There would be talk of farming matters and 'long clock-clicking silences'. Then granddad would suggest a song and they'd be off into melody, with everybody joining in. There was little fear of the old songs dying as long as the Coppers still remembered the words and the tunes.

Bob also tells of the Coppers being invited to sing for the 'gentry' at their houses. And similar invitations came from the master of the local hunt, to sing Christmas carols on Boxing Day around a steaming bowl of punch.

After *A Song for Every Season,* other books followed – *Early to Rise, Songs and Southern Breezes, Bob Copper's Sussex* and *Across Sussex with Belloc.* Next to be published will be Bob's memoirs.

Over the years the village of Rottingdean has seen many changes, with housing eating up the green fields where the Coppers used to work, and cars polluting the country lanes. But the songs go on. The family of singing Coppers now comprises Bob, his son and daughter, John and Jill, Jill's husband Jon Dudley, and Bob's grandchildren Lucy, Ben, Tom, Mark, Andrew and Sean.

In 1994 the Coppers embarked on the first of several American tours; in 2000 alone they made three tours to the US and in all have visited twenty-three states. Over the years they have sung in the Library of Congress in Washington, at summer camps, down-town folk clubs and concert halls. But where, in England, folk-singing and drinking are inextricably linked, in America the performances are 'dry'. 'Over there, someone defined a folk club as somewhere where you have fourteen different kinds of cheesecake,' Jon says.

What keeps the Coppers on the road, still singing through the centuries? Their rewards are not enormous. They are no pop stars and nor would they want to be. They do it quite simply because it's a fun thing to do. They enjoy each other's company. It's an extra family bonding and they feel a responsibility to hand down the singing tradition to the next generation as it was bequeathed to them.

The Coppers love a drink, a laugh and a song. Asked how he'd like to be remembered, Bob says quite simply: 'As a happy man, able to pass on some of the happy times to the next generation.'

*From the left, John Copper, Jill Dudley, Bob Copper, Jon Dudley*

# Follies Galore!

## JOHN (MAD JACK) FULLER (1757-1834)

Of all the characters in this book, perhaps John Fuller, known as Mad Jack, left the most substantial memorials to his life on earth. These are his six follies situated around the village of Brightling, where he lived. Jack had two of the prerequisites for being a folly builder. He was the village squire, a position of some power. And he was rich.

The Brightling estate descended through the family to Mad Jack from his grandfather, John Fuller. It was John who changed the name Brightling Park to Rose Hill in honour of his wife, Elizabeth Rose, daughter of Fulke Rose of Jamaica. Jack's own parents were cousins – Henry Fuller, rector of South Stoneham, Hampshire, and Frances Fuller, daughter of Thomas Fuller of Park Gate, Catsfield, in Sussex.

The parson died when Jack was only five. At the age of ten, he was sent to Eton, where he remained until 1774. He didn't follow school with university but may well have done what many rich young men enjoyed – the grand tour of Europe.

In 1777, at the age of twenty, Jack inherited the Brightling estate from his uncle who had the unusual Christian name of Rose. Along with the estate came the family's Sussex iron works, and sugar plantations in Jamaica. This fortune was added to in the following year when his mother died and left him more property and money.

In 1780, when Parliament was the province of the wealthy and influential, Jack was elected the MP for Southampton. To be closer to the House of Commons, he bought a grand house in London's Wimpole Street.

In 1790, at the age of thirty-three, Jack proposed marriage to twenty-four-year-old Susan Thrale. After she turned him down Jack reacted with bad grace. In a fit of pique, he tried to embarrass Susan by having a London prostitute follow her around Tunbridge Wells, where she had gone to take the waters. Following this, Jack never again proposed to anyone but seems to have enjoyed a healthy sex life with the likes of housemaids.

In 1796, Jack filled the post of High Sheriff for Sussex, for a year. Then, in 1801, he was returned as a Tory MP for Sussex, a position he gained partly by paying the 'travelling expenses' of those who voted for him.

Jack, who weighed more than twenty-two stones, had a voracious appetite. He was big and bluff – another nickname was Hippopotamus – and had a loud, booming voice. He wore his hair in a pigtail, on top of which he sported a powdered wig. His coarse and colourful language and his obstreperous behaviour earned him the reputation of court jester in the House of Commons.

*From Henry Singleton's portrait of John Fuller*

He had several rows with the Speaker, calling him 'an insignificant little man in the wig'. At least twice, Mad Jack had to be ejected from the House. And during one dreary debate, he insisted on booming out the joys and glories of living in Sussex. There were all sorts of stories about him; one was that he drove a coach and six into a crowded House of Commons.

William Pit the Younger offered him a peerage. Jack, however, declined the honour, telling Pitt that: 'I was born Jack Fuller and Jack Fuller I'll die.' For this he earned the further nickname of Honest John.

But Jack's career as a parliamentarian really came to an end during a stormy and acrimonious debate on February 28, 1810. The confrontation concerned a military expedition that had gone badly wrong. A force of 40,000 British troops had been sent to the Continent to destroy Napoleon's base at Antwerp and to raise a Dutch revolt. It failed on all counts and ended so disastrously that of a garrison of 15,000 troops, 7,000 died of malaria and 3,000 were permanently incapacitated.

Jack took this as a plot against king and country and became increasingly agitated, his booming voice resounding around the chamber. His language became foul and he issued insults in all directions. The Speaker demanded that he leave the House and at first Jack complied and left the chamber, escorted by the Sergeant at Arms. Then, struggling free, he again burst into the chamber 'causing great commotion'. This was too much for the Speaker, who ordered him to be placed in one of the cells in the Palace Yard.

The next day Jack made profuse apologies to the House and he was released from his cell. But the experience had had an effect on Fuller. Parliamentary business lost its glitter and in 1812 he left Parliament for ever.

Jack now needed something to replace politics and he became increasingly interested in the arts and sciences. Among visitors to Rose Hill were the artist, JMW Turner, and the architect, Robert Smirke. Jack bought a number of Turner paintings showing Sussex scenes and commissioned Smirke to design his follies.

Of the six follies that Jack built, only one was for a practical purpose and this was the Observatory. It is also the only building for which plans survive. Smirke designed it in 1810 and it was completed in 1818. Jack, an amateur astronomer, equipped the building with the most sophisticated equipment available, including a camera-obscura. The Observatory gave a commanding view over the surrounding countryside, as well as skywards, and from here, Rose Hill staff could spot Jack's coach returning from London, and they could prepare a warm welcome.

The Rotunda Temple was also probably designed by Smirke around 1810. Set on top of a small slope in the middle of Brightling Park, it is built with Doric pillars in the Grecian style. There were several stories regarding its use, among them that it was a place for the squire to entertain his lady friends. Another was that it was somewhere to store smuggled goods, or even a place where smugglers gathered and plotted their next run.

It was characteristic of Jack that when he learned that plans were afoot to demolish Bodiam Castle, he leapt to the rescue. A Hastings construction company wanted to buy the castle to use it as a source of building materials. Jack bought the castle and had it renovated. It was said that he monitored the work from another of his follies, the thirty-five foot, two-storey Tower, some twelve feet in diameter.

Another tower, the Sugar Loaf (it resembled the cone shape in which sugar was delivered to grocers of the time), is some thirty-five feet high on a circular base fifteen feet in diameter, situated on the south-west side of Brightling Park. The story goes that it was put up in a single night to help Jack win a wager. While away from home, Jack bet a friend that, from Rose Hill, he could see the spire of St Giles' church in the next village of Dallington. But when he returned home, he realised that he had forgotten that there was a hill between his house and the church, blocking the view. Undaunted, he had the Sugerloaf tower erected so that from the top he could see St Giles' spire.

Who knows? The story could well be true. After all, experts say that the Sugerloaf is built only of stones and mud, which suggests that it was put up in a great hurry!

Just like the ancient pharaohs, Mad Jack made preparations for the after-life, twenty-four years before he died. His mausoleum was to be a twenty-five foot high pyramid in Brightling Parish churchyard. For permission to build it, Jack struck a bargain with the vicar. Jack would have a stone wall built around the churchyard at his own expense. The deal was agreed. The vicar had his wall, Jack his pyramid. For many years after Jack's death, local rumour had it that their local pharaoh sat propped up in a chair with a table spread lavishly with food and a bottle of claret within reach. The floor was spread with broken glass to deter the devil – who would cut his tender hooves if he approached.

Alas, like so many stories about Mad Jack, it proved to be a complete fabrication. Some years ago the rotting wooden door was taken out and an iron grill put in its place. The late squire, it was discovered, lay buried under the pyramid in the conventional manner.

Another wild story is connected with the pyramid. It seems that Mad Jack advertised twice for a hermit to occupy the structure. The conditions of employment were that the hermit must not wash, shave or cut his hair for a whole year. After that, Jack would make him 'a gentleman for life'. Apparently, there were no takers.

Brightling Needle may have been designed by Robert Smirke and may have been erected in 1815 to celebrate the British victory at Waterloo. It is very similar to Smirke's Wellington Memorial in Phoenix Park, Dublin, but unlike the latter, it has no inscription. Perhaps it was just a whim, built for no particular reason

*The Sugar Loaf*

whatsoever, in the true spirit of the folly-builders.

Throughout his life, Jack was responsible for many generous donations. In 1820, he gave the largest barrel organ in Britain, in full working order, to his local church. It came with its own gallery. On another occasion, he gave a peal of eight bells to the church.

Further afield, Honest Jack founded the Royal Institution of Great Britain in 1799, with premises in Albermarle Street, London, its purpose being 'the promotion, diffusion, and extension of science and useful knowledge'. He set up two professorships which he described as his 'only two legitimate children'. In 1803, he donated £50 for the institution reference library, and in 1819 he gave it a volume of *Views of Sussex* by Turner, followed in 1826 by four patent globe lamps. He also presented his portrait painted by Henry Singleton. In gratitude, the Royal Institution arranged to have a bust of him on the premises. The inscription read: 'John Fuller who gave ten thousand pounds for the promotion of science in the Royal Institution'.

Mad Jack Fuller died at the age of 77, in 1834. He was much mourned. For in his life he had added colour and excitement to those around him. He had given the unemployed work in building his follies and other structures. His generosity spread from his own village to the heart of London. (There is even a tale of him throwing golden guineas out of his bedroom window when he was shaving). And for the county of Sussex, he has left his own peculiar remembrances, his follies.

He would not have been pleased that, after his death, a subsequent owner changed the name of the estate back to Brightling Park.

If he was mad, it was an attractive kind of madness.

✳ ✳ ✳

# A Life Devoted to Animal Rescue

## PAULINE GRANT (1936-)

Ever wondered what happens to the racehorse that can no longer race? The pet donkey whose owners become bored by it? Or a pony that's too old to be ridden? The unlucky ones go to the knacker's yard, are sold off to the highest bidder, and may even end up enduring the cruelties of a circus or fun fair. On the other hand, the really lucky ones are rescued by a charity like the Sussex Horse Rescue Trust at Uckfield, where they are cared for and given a happy retirement. The trust is owned and run by Pauline Grant and her story is one of courage and determination and the conviction that she would win through no matter what.

Pauline, an attractive, friendly woman with plenty to say for herself, has spent a lifetime endeavouring to improve the lot of animals. She has been at the forefront of those protesting against the export of live animals, has been a member of the League Against

*Pauline Grant with some of the animals in her care*

Cruel Sports since she was thirteen, is sympathetic to hunt saboteurs, and engaged in rescuing and rehabilitating animals in her own sanctuary since the early 1960s.

Pauline was born Pauline Tulley in Cuckfield, Sussex, on August 3, 1936, the only child of a businessman owner of a chain of post office-stores. She had a comfortable childhood albeit a lonely one, as her mother had died at an early age. Pauline was brought up mainly by housekeepers, and remembers no 'home life'. It was because she was so lonely, she said, that she first became interested in animals.

Pauline was educated at St Clare's, a private school in Haywards Heath. When she looked around for a suitable career there was nobody to guide her, so on leaving school at fifteen she went to work for a hairdresser.

Pauline married at seventeen to Jeff Munn and was divorced ten years later. She married again, to Rene Grant, and this also ended in divorce. Left to bring up four children on her own, three boys and a girl, she looked around for a job she could combine with child care. It was around this time – the early 1960s – that the idea of an animal rescue centre came to her. If you look after animals, she reckoned, the children can come with you, and enjoy doing it.

She was living in the village of Bolney in a spacious house given to her by her father, but there was no land. So after meeting all the local farmers, Pauline toted her begging bowl around the village. She was rewarded with fifty acres of free grazing land at Heron Farm, Ashurst, given by various land owners including a branch of the Guinness family. She then set to erecting fences and providing water for her animals. Her first rescue was a shire horse she had to hand-rear. The foal's mother had been put in a just-creosoted stable, licked the creosote and died.

In the 1970s Pauline met Eileen Bezet, who was heavily engaged in protests to stop the transportation of live animals for slaughter abroad. Together, they were involved in a great deal of undercover work at horse sales, docks, ferries and Moslem ritual slaughterhouses abroad. Photographic evidence of gross maltreatment was given to the British Veterinary Association's Welfare Committee, Dartmoor Livestock Association and other bodies. By the end of the 1970s, protest against the live trade was well established with many supporters. What wasn't being addressed was the terrible suffering and neglect of horses and donkeys in Britain, and Pauline decided to direct her energies in this direction.

She began to recruit volunteers to help with fund-raising. She petitioned local councils on the treatment of rodeo horses, circus animals and other issues. In June 1988 she rescued Clara, a pony owned by the Sandhurst Travelling Circus, which lived happily at the sanctuary for eleven years. Clara suffered from ringbone, a painful bone deformity attributed to having performed on her hind legs in the circus, and in 1999 she was mercifully put down.

Realising that rescue was to be her life's work, Pauline decided to form the Sussex Horse Rescue Trust as a registered charity. But to do this, she needed space. She sold her house and with the money bought Heron Farm, at Ashurst, near Steyning in West Sussex, with ninety-six acres of grazing land. There was just one drawback. There was no house on the land, just a mobile home for herself, two of her sons and the many house pets they were constantly acquiring.

Pauline had assistance from the inmates of Ford open prison, about half-an-hour away. She'd been advised to steer clear of rapists, burglars, and arsonists so she asked for murderers every time. Like John Mortimer, she says that most murderers have committed the only crime they will ever commit.

The family put up with this for six years, despite the cramped conditions and the growing number of animals. Then in 1992, a friend and trustee, Phyllis Creak, died, leaving the trust a considerable legacy.

After searching for more than a year, Pauline found Hempstead Farm, on the rural outskirts of Uckfield. It was badly neglected – both farm and house – but it did have a lot of potential. The large house was in desperate need of renovation but Pauline decided that this must wait until the animals had all been accommodated satisfactorily. They settled here in 1994.

Rescued animals coming to the trust are by no means free of cost; many are bought. A retired racehorse could cost £900 and several hundred pounds for other animals is not uncommon. The watchwords of the charity are Rescue, Rehabilitation, and Loan. Those who want to take an animal on loan are strictly vetted and a list of conditions is attached. Pauline or her staff also make regular visits to inspect the living conditions of all loaned animals.

Pauline has a staff of six helpers and the number of animals in her care is impressive. At the time of writing there are some eighty horses, ponies and donkeys, two llamas, two pot-bellied pigs as well as numerous chickens, geese, cats and dogs. On top of this a number of other animals are on loan – as many as 200 horses and donkeys, goats and sheep.

Pauline was once asked what was her biggest extravagance. She put it neatly in three words – wasting time sleeping.

# 'Call Me a Spectre Inspector'

## ANDREW GREEN (1927-

A ndrew Green's first brush with the paranormal very nearly cost him his life. It was in 1944 when Andrew was seventeen. His father, who was chief housing officer for Ealing Borough Council, had the job of selecting and commandeering empty properties in which to store furniture recovered from bombed houses. One evening he asked his son if he would be interested in seeing a haunted house and Andrew jumped at the idea. The house (now demolished) was in Montpelier Road and had been empty since 1934. It had also been the notorious setting for at least one murder, and some twenty suicides who had jumped from a high tower attached to the house.

It was when father and son climbed the tower that it happened. The top of the tower was about seventy feet from the ground but to Andrew at the highest point, it felt as if it was merely a foot or so away. He had a strong, inexplicable sensation that he wanted to get down into the back garden below. He felt himself being drawn over the parapet and he started to step down. At the last moment, as he was poised between life and certain death, his father grabbed him from behind. Was this the same sensation experienced by the twenty suicides, and had they had nobody to pull them back? We'll never know but he could have so easily been the twenty-first suicide.

This haunted house had something else in store and it was an incident that has been much publicised wherever Andrew's name has been mentioned – in books, in the newspapers, on radio and on television. After his split-second escape from death, the teenager was anxious to take a photograph of the house to show his friends. He snapped the back of the empty house but when the print came back from the processors, an image was seen that had not been noticed when Andrew took the photograph. It was the figure of a young girl, approximately the age of the twelve-year-old who had committed suicide there in 1886.

The film was checked by Ilford and Kodak. Both laboratories confirmed that the film had not been tampered with. They also made the point that sometimes film will record something that isn't visible to the naked eye.

In 1949, Andrew founded the Ealing Society for the Investigation of Psychic Phenomena and served as its chairman until 1953. He was co-founder of the National Federation of Psychic Research Societies in 1951, and the Institute of Service Management in 1960. In the late 1960s, Andrew's researches established that children of seven had the highest perception of phenomena but this diminishes with age.

But what exactly is a ghost? Andrew pointed out to me that NASA satellites, travelling round the earth, are photographing 'ghosts' all the time. Their cameras are picking up heat images that were in place, minutes, hours or even months before. Some of these images are of people, and some of these must have died. So a number of the NASA photographs could be described as of so-called 'ghosts'.

He then got rather more technical. These ghosts, he explained, 'are images formed of electromagnetic energy between 380 and 440 "millimicrons" of the infra-red portion of the light spectrum. The 'ghosts' are created by people on learning of the sudden and unexpected death of a loved one. They do not have personalities or intelligence but are images, sometimes of domestic animals, which had been members of the family.'

Andrew went into his theories in some detail. When, for example, a man or woman receives a severe and intense shock on hearing of the death of a spouse or partner, he or she has an immediate image of the dead person, where last seen. It could be at home or miles away. It doesn't matter. The image remains at the site and can be seen by anyone approaching it, but whose mind at the time is inactive. That witness unconsciously transfers heat to the area which recharges the apparition and it becomes visible. 'This explains,' Andrew goes on, 'why a chill in the air is so often reported by those who see ghosts.'

Colours of phantoms appear to have faded if they remain unseen for a long time. He also says, surprisingly, that some seventy per cent of witnessed ghosts are of living people, for somebody doesn't have to die to create an image.

Many apparitions can be created unconsciously by imagination or a strong desire to be in another location. A successful exorcism can perhaps alleviate the stress of witnessing an apparition or a ghost, if called upon.

Both smells and sounds can also be recreated unknowingly at the time of the haunting. They actually become embedded in the building materials and can be regenerated by just the right conditions of moisture and temperature.

Andrew is an agnostic and dismisses theories of life after death because they can not be proven to his satisfaction.

He doesn't perform any ghost-ridding ceremonies, and is irritated by people who, although aiming at helping those seriously affected by

*Andrew Green*

hysteria, imagination, faulty medication or some alleged example of paranormal experience, carry out a totally unauthorised pseudo-rite. He also objects to an 'approved' exorcism, involving authority from a bishop, without initially checking basic human beliefs of the victims.

Has Andrew actually seen any ghosts? He cites two possible experiences. The first occurred just after the war when he was staying with friends in Devon and awoke to find a fox terrier in his bedroom. It stayed there only momentarily then it was gone. He mentioned this to the family who said they had no dog. But the previous residents had owned a fox terrier that was run over by a car and killed. During its lifetime it had been allowed to sleep in the bedroom occupied by Andrew.

The second ghost appeared to be human. Andrew, then aged about twenty-four, was staying in a Worthing boarding house. He woke at eight in the morning to see a small boy in old fashioned clothing standing by the bed. The boy put down a cup of tea. Andrew took a sip and found the tea cold; the boy vanished. The landlady later said there were no children in the house. However, a fellow guest explained that several other people who had stayed in that room experienced a similar visitation. The landlady, not wanting to put guests off, usually explained that it was she who had left the tea by the bedside the night before.

Andrew Green was born on July 28, 1927, in Ealing, London, when his father was serving as an officer in the Metropolitan Police. He went to Bordeston Grammar School, and in 1951 married Hazel Hunter; they divorced in 1971. In 1979 he married Norah Bridget Cawthorne (née Styles) and they live in an eighteenth century cottage, near Robertsbridge, in Sussex.

After three years of National Service in the Lifeguards (Household Cavalry), Andrew was in turn a development chemist, office administrator, advertising and publicity manager, publications editor and adult tutor. From 1968 to 1972 Andrew ran his own publishing company, Malcolm Publications, which produced house journals and souvenir travel material.

He retired officially in 1997, after twenty-five years' lecturing in educational establishments. He has assisted various councils and authorities and private individuals with investigations of a para-psychological nature, written some six books including *Ghost Hunting, a Practical Guide,* and presented courses in several colleges. He is a thin, courteous man with an impressive wave of grey hair.

Andrew has appeared frequently in the media, in Britain and abroad. Perhaps the greatest barrage of publicity occurred in April 1996, when he was commissioned by the Royal Albert Hall in London to carry out an investigative project into alleged phenomena being experienced by security staff. It attracted enormous publicity and news of his investigations were reported across Europe. There were enquiries from as far away as Mexico, France, Canada, America and Australia.

Reports of spectral apparitions, strange noises and sudden chills had plagued the corridors of the Albert Hall for sixty years. Two young women in Victorian dress had been seen, talking animatedly and giggling, then vanishing in front of the kitchen doors on the lower ground floor. Another phantom visitor was claimed to be that of Father Willis, a stooped figure in a black skull cap who often inspected the musical organ that he himself had built in the nineteenth century. There was also the hint of sex with which to spice other stories. Going further back in time, when Gore House stood on the site, the Count d'Orsay ran a brothel in the basement. And long ago, two workmen had met their deaths there, while diverting an underground river.

Andrew arrived at the Albert Hall with a case full of detecting equipment which included a high-frequency response and recording unit, night scope, anti-static pistol, digital thermometer, electricity detector, and assorted cameras. Except for one hour during the eighteen-hour vigil, he was accompanied by an enthusiastic press pack, who spent the night with him in the area where a 'sighting' had last been made.

But for all this, Andrew himself could have predicted the outcome. He has always said 'you never see a ghost when you're looking for one'. And alas, in this case, he was proved right. This may also be the reason why Andrew Green has seen so very few ghosts of any kind. If anyone needs help with a problem in dealing with any aspect of the paranormal, he is available, though aware that what you believe is your own reality.

# The Indian Brave from Hastings

## GREY OWL/ARCHIE BELANEY (1888-1938)

**P**icture a theatre in 1935 Britain. On to the stage steps a long, lean, weatherbeaten Indian brave dressed in buckskins and moccasins, with long braided hair. While the audience is hushed, he raises his palm. 'My name is Wa-sha-quonasin, He-who-walks-by-night – Grey Owl. I come in peace.'

His voice is clear and melodious, with the slight guttural tone of an Indian. He speaks of the Canadian wilderness that is his home. Of the Indians and white trappers who live there. Of the struggle to survive the bone-chilling winters. He talks of the native animals he once trapped and killed and now saves, and how he came to the decision to devote his life to conservation.

The audience sits spellbound – as they have all over the country. The planned two-week tour has been expanded to four months, over which time he gives some 200 lectures, to total audiences of more than a quarter of a million. People also buy his books, at the rate of more than 1000 a week. He has earned a fortune.

Then barely three years later, in April 1938, Grey Owl dies, aged forty-nine. The body is hardly cold before headlines everywhere accuse him of being one of the century's greatest literary hoaxers. Grey Owl is not the half-breed he always claimed to be but an Englishman from Hastings called Archie Belaney. And a bigamist at that.

True, Grey Owl or Archie Belaney never claimed to be a saint. He had fooled a lot of people with his story of having a Scottish father and an Indian mother. And when he was described as a full blood, he never denied it. True also is that at the time when he had come home from the the First World War, he had often been drunk and in trouble with the law. And he did go through an official marriage ceremony with at least three women.

Archie Stansfield Belaney was born on September 18, 1888, at 32 St James's Road, Hastings. His father, George, was always pursuing get-rich-quick schemes and never really settling anywhere. When he married Archie's mother, Kittie Morris, it was his second marriage and she was reputedly only thirteen (the age of consent at the time). Then shortly after Archie's birth, George went off to America and his mother married again. The boy was left to grow up with his grandmother and two aunts, Ada and Carrie Belaney, in Hastings.

In a sense, Archie was always an Indian. As a boy, he played at being one in St Helen's Wood and among the scrub of the foreshore at Pett. From the time he could read, he knew all about Indians and dreamed of the day he would become one. Other boys were similarly inspired by the comics with their tales of Sitting Bull, and dreamed of living in the American wild west. The difference with Archie was that he never lost those dreams.

*Grey Owl in 1931*

After working briefly as a clerk with a Hastings firm, he sailed from Liverpool to Halifax in 1906. Upon arrival, he travelled to Lake Temagami in Ontario, where a settler taught him the art of wilderness trapping. He got to know the Ojibway Indians living on Bear Island and learnt all he could, listening to the elders telling stories in the evenings, and hunting with the young braves. He ceased to speak English and became identified with the Ojibway. He spoke of the *shag-a-nash,* the white man, as though he belonged to another race.

In 1910 he embarked on the first of at least three marriages. Angele Eguana was a maiden from the local tribe. He could speak fairly fluent Ojibway, had braided his long hair and his skin had darkened by constant exposure to all weathers. Angele had a child by him and it seemed that he had settled down. But the wanderlust emerged again and in 1912 he told his wife that he taken a job as a fire ranger and would be away some time. He returned in six years.

He worked out of Biscotasing – trapping in the winter and working with the rangers in the summer. He virtually cut himself off from the white world and lived as the Indians did. He also earned something of a reputation as a heavy drinker and a man handy with a knife. It was at this time too that he began to show his powers of oratory. The stories he told in the evenings were often profane and – just as he had done as a small boy – he loved to shock.

In 1915 he went off to war with the Canadian army. As a sharp-shooter, he was employed in Flanders as a sniper. He was wounded in the foot, suffered from gas poisoning and was brought to England to convalesce. He met many old friends, including a girl called Florence Holmes. She fell for his charms and they married in the Church-in-the-Wood, in Hollington, St Leonards. However he spent even less time with his second wife than with his first. Their marriage ended abruptly in divorce, and in 1917 he returned to the wild country of Bisco.

But Canada was not the country he had left a couple of years earlier. Fur prices had risen and hoards of get-rich-quick trappers were everywhere. Their wholesale methods of slaughter had always been anathema to Grey Owl (as he now called himself): the new breed of hunter cared little about sparing pups and pregnant females. In addition, great new roads had been cut into the forest, forcing the Indians further into the wilderness.

Confronted by ruthlessness, Archie replied in kind, trapping more animals than anyone else. Then in 1925, someone entered his life who was to change it forever. This was a beautiful, nineteen-year-old Iroquois girl called Anahareo, whom Archie nicknamed Pony. She brought out the best side of Archie – the little boy who loved to watch animals and not to kill them. They were married Indian fashion and lived as Indians.

His change of life began one day after a mother beaver had been drowned in one of his traps, leaving behind two helpless kittens. Grey Owl raised his gun to shoot the kittens when he saw the anguish in Anahareo's eyes. Slowly he put down the rifle and turned away. His wife stepped forward, gently nestled the two kittens under her shirt and took them home. MacGinnis and MacGinty, as the kittens were called, had entered their lives and were soon to be immortalised in print.

Archie planned to sell the pair of kittens until one night, as he was lying in bed, MacGinnis jumped up on to the bed beside him. At first, the baby beaver gave himself a good wash then climbed up on the trapper's chest and settled himself down for the night. This was the turning point. There was no more talk of selling their new companions.

Gradually, a new idea came to the man who had always trapped and killed for a living. He noticed that the number of beavers in the wild was declining. Could they be saved from extinction? So he began what he would always be remembered for – conservation. It was a new concept and Grey Owl was among its pioneers.

In the spring, MacGinnis and MacGinty ran away for good but before Grey Owl and Pony had time to mourn, the young beavers were replaced by two more – called Jelly Roll and Rawhide. These animals and their adventures were also soon to find their way into print. At first, Grey Owl sent articles to *Country Life,* which were accepted and paid for. Publication in other magazines followed, in Canada and England.

By the time of his first book, *The Men of the Last Frontier,* published in 1931, he had become an Indian writer. His style adopted colloquialisms and grammatical misuses, in an effort to make his readers think that he was in truth a half-breed Indian. In this guise, more books followed.

In the same year, Grey Owl and Anahareo moved to Lake Ajawaan, in Prince Albert National Park, Saskatchewan. The Canadian government had heard of their conservation schemes and did all they could to help. The eloquent Indian was offered the position of naturalist with a brief to start a beaver colony. Some half a dozen nature films were made of this.

It was also in 1931 that Grey Owl gave his first major public lecture, as the guest of the Canadian Forestry Association's annual convention. Grey Owl was introduced as a full-blooded Indian and his biographer and friend, Lovat Dickson, maintains that Archie was caught up in the whole business of his promotion as an Indian. He felt his conservationist message would come through more forcefully from an Indian than from a white man.

Lovat Dickson arranged several British tours between 1935 and 1937. Among the highlights was a visit to Buckingham Palace to meet

George VI and the two princesses, Elizabeth and Margaret. The future queen was a keen reader of Grey Owl's books and as the story teller was about to conclude his talk to them, she jumped up and cried, 'Oh, do go on!' Later, taking his leave of the King, Grey Owl shook him by the hand and said 'Goodbye brother. I'll be seeing you.'

The 1930s was a dismal decade into which Grey Owl stepped like a breath of fresh air. He gave his listeners hope that somewhere a better, simpler life existed with real values that the old world seemed to be losing.

At the end of his final lecture tour, Grey Owl returned to Beaver Lodge and renewed his acquaintance with Jelly Roll and Rawhide. Then on April 10, 1938, he called the Park Office at Waskesiu to say that he was feeling ill and was picked up and driven to the Prince Albert Hospital. At midnight on April 12 he sank into a coma and died the next morning, April 13, aged forty-nine.

One of Grey Owl's friends, Laya Retenburg, spoke of him some thirty years after his death. She said, 'I still see and feel the almost magical impact his presence and message had upon audiences, large and small. I literally saw him capture the attention and often the hearts of the very people he criticised.'

In some ways, Grey Owl was a man out of his time. Years before the world cared about the needless killing of wildlife or the preservation of the wilderness, Grey Owl made people listen to his message. Anahareo lived until she was eighty. When asked how she remembered Archie, she said: 'To me he was an Indian and one of the best men I'd ever met.'

Her husband couldn't have asked for a better epitaph.

# The 'Perfect Murders'

## John George Haigh (1909-1949)

Haigh's usual method of killing his victims was to shoot them at close range, make an incision in the neck, collect the blood in a glass and drink it (he said it filled him with elation and a sense of power). He would then dissolve the body in a drum of sulphuric acid and, so he thought, leave no evidence. In the murderer's mind it was the perfect crime.

This was disclosed at the Lewes Assizes Court in July 1949, at one of the most sensational murder trials to ever take place in Sussex. And whether he really did drink the victims' blood will never be known. Many believed that Haigh simply added that to the other evidence so that he would be declared insane and would cheat the hangman.

Haigh was not just a murderer but a forger and confidence man of extraordinary ability. He fooled everyone - lawyers, bankers, policemen, business men, factory owners and engineers, even close friends and those he lived with.

John George Haigh was born in Stanford, Lincolnshire, in 1909, the lonely only son of Plymouth Brethren, who denied the boy sport, entertainment, newspapers and radio; reading was restricted to the Bible. He was, however, given a good education and as a teenager, seemed a well adjusted young man ready for a fine career. By his early twenties, he was well-spoken, well-dressed and well-groomed.

Haigh, though, was an inveterate liar, also a skilled forger. At twenty-one he formed a company in Leeds, which was involved in underwriting and advertising, and as an estate agency. At first things went well until, in 1932, Leeds CID charged him with three cases of attempted false pretences. To the police, he must have appeared well dressed, well spoken and respectable, and he was dismissed under the Indictable Offences Act.

In 1933 he floated another company for selling advertising on large electric signs. At the same time he was employed by a Leeds motor insurance company that also ran a hire-purchase subsidiary. He had the responsibility of boosting the hire-purchase side of the

*John George Haigh*

business. He was popular, and considered good at his work.

Then, after eighteen months, it was discovered that Haigh was involved in fraudulent hire-purchase transactions. He still lived at home and his father was summoned. Haigh senior agreed to make good all the money his son had obtained under false pretences, and the culprit was fired.

Several months later Haigh married a Stockport model, Beatrice Hamer, a girl he had known for only a very short time. Neither parents liked the union.

Then, to everyone's surprise he joined his old firm's sister company. How he had persuaded the company to take him on, nobody could say. It was likely to have been the old Haigh charm. However, after about fifteen months he was again caught out, and convicted of conspiracy to defraud, obtaining money by false pretences and attempting to obtain money by fraud. He was sentenced to fifteen months. While he was in prison his wife gave birth to a daughter, who was later adopted. Haigh never saw the baby, nor lived with his wife again.

More crime followed and on June 10, 1941, he was given a twenty-one month stretch with hard labour at Lincoln. Books in the prison library showed him how to change from a fraudster to a killer. In the tinsmith's shop, he found that whole mice dissolved in sulphuric acid, leaving no trace and he started to plan the 'perfect murder' that would leave no body.

After his release, he obtained a job in Crawley with a light-engineering firm and found digs in Northgate Road. But for his next planned crimes, he needed the anonymity of London. He took lodgings in Queens' Gate and formed an 'engineering company' with fictional branches. A basement at 79 Gloucester Road provided the perfect place to carry out his killings. He stocked the basement with sulphuric acid and various implements.

His first victim was an old acquaintance he ran into in the Goat, a pub in Kensington High Street. This was William McSwan, a man of considerable means, who was planning to 'disappear' to avoid call-up to the forces (Haigh, by one means or another, managed to avoid call-up). McSwan, known as Mac, wanted a place of storage and Haigh was quick to offer his basement.

On Saturday September 9, 1944, the two men had a meal at the Goat, when Haigh suggested that he show Mac his basement. Once there, Haigh sneaked up behind his victim with a large piece of lead piping and smashed it down onto his head. Mac fell unconscious and died within minutes.

After taking everything of value from Mac's clothing, he forced the body into an oil drum. He had purchased several carboys of sulphuric acid and transferred about ten gallons into the drum with a bucket. He returned on the Monday to pour the unpleasant, reeking remains down the drain in the centre of the floor.

Haigh now approached the victim's elderly parents with the story that Mac had gone to Scotland to avoid National Service and that he, Haigh, would be pleased to act as rent collector for Mac's five rented houses until his friend returned. Haigh made several trips to Scotland, from where he dispatched a series of chatty letters, perfectly forged in Mac's handwriting.

On the morning of Friday, July 6, 1945, two more oil drums waited in the gruesome basement. Haigh persuaded Mac's father, Donald McSwan, that his son was returning, and lured him to the basement. Donald died from a blow to the head, and the same fate befell his wife a little later. They were packed, side by side, into the two oil drums of acid.

Friends and neighbours were informed that the family had made a sudden decision to emigrate to America, leaving Haigh with power of attorney. He sold all the McSwans' personal effects and all five houses. Haigh was so plausible that even the conveyancing solicitors suspected nothing. The sales raised some £6,000, a small fortune in post-war England.

It took the mass-murderer two years of extravagant living to get through the McSwan inheritance and by August, 1947, Haigh was down to an overdraft of £25. He closed the London basement and moved the tools of his deadly trade to a small workshop in Leopold Road, Crawley. It was lent to him by a partner he had financed while in the money. The new premises were not as private as the Gloucester Road basement but by this time, Haigh was supremely confident.

His next victims – and the chance to replenish his finances – were a rich middle-aged couple, Dr Archie Henderson and his wife, Rose. Haigh posed as a would-be buyer of their house and he was soon a regular guest. He had the ability to earn others' trust and before very long he had Archie's complete confidence.

The workshop, Haigh's so-called Union Group Engineering, was now stocked with three glass carboys of sulphuric acid, a stirrup pump for pumping in the acid, long rubber gloves, a rubber apron, a heavy raincoat, and thigh-length rubber boots. Two recent acquisitions – a wartime gas mask and a .38 Enfield revolver – had been stolen from the Henderson's flat while they were away.

The Hendersons planned a few days on holiday in Broadstairs, and at the Metropole Hotel, Brighton. Calling at the hotel, Haigh persuaded Archie to accompany him to Union Group Engineering to discuss a new business venture. The killer used Archie's own Enfield to shoot him. A few hours later, Archie's wife, Rose, shared the same fate. Haigh rang the Metropole in a woman's voice, informing the management that Mrs Henderson would not be returning that night.

The murderer enjoyed a good night's sleep at Kensington and returned to Crawley early the next morning to dispose of the bodies. His new equipment helped to protect him from acid spills and the deadly fumes. He tipped the remains into the yard and wrote the Hendersons' initials, AH and RH, in his diary.

The murder was one thing but convincing the Hendersons' friends and family to accept Haigh's lies was another. But Haigh smoothly convinced them all. With a collection of forged documents and letters, he gained all the Hendersons' worldly goods, amounting to £7,771. It took the killer six months – to January 1949 – to fritter it away.

For some time, Haigh's neighbour in the Onslow Court Hotel had been a wealthy, intelligent, and attractive sixty-nine-year-old woman, Olive Durand-Deacon. She proposed a business deal involving manufacturing plastic finger nails – the perfect combination of her money and Haigh's engineering skill. Haigh restocked his so-called business premises and just after lunch on Friday, February 18, 1949, drove Mrs Durand-Deacon to the site for her murder. In no time, Haigh's former dinner-time companion was sizzling away in a bath of acid.

But this time, Haigh's luck was beginning to run out. He raised £110 by selling his victim's jewellery and left her expensive fur coat at the dry cleaners. Now for her £36,000 in investments . . .

Haigh didn't know it yet but his days were already numbered. Some forty-eight hours after Mrs Durand-Deacon's disappearance from the hotel, her best friend and fellow hotel guest, Constance Lane, decided to go to the police. Hearing of her intentions over breakfast, Haigh volunteered to go with her.

At the police station, the woman police sergeant took an instant dislike to Haigh and when she discovered from the hotel that Haigh had been tardy in paying his bills, she sent a personal memo to the head of Chelsea CID, Detective Chief Inspector Shelley Symes. Symes checked police records and soon discovered Haigh's long list of fraud convictions.

It wasn't long before the police discovered Haigh's 'business premises' at Crawley. Along with the murder equipment, they found Haigh's briefcase containing documents related to his killings. The dry cleaning receipt revealed the latest victim's expensive fur coat.

Haigh, taken in for questioning, realised that the game was up. His confession lasted some six hours. At first, he almost boasted of his success in destroying the evidence: 'How can you prove murder if there is no body?'

But even in that he was wrong. From the yard outside the Leopold Road premises, forensic officers removed 475 pounds of soil. They found bits of bone, twenty-eight pounds of body fat, other fragments and undissolved gall stones. A dentist was able to identify the dead woman's dentures.

The trial took place at Lewes Assizes in July 1949, with mass publicity from the press. Haigh attempted unsuccessfully to plead insanity, citing his habit of drinking the victims' blood. Newspaper headlines referred to him as 'the Vampire'. The jury took only seventeen minutes to find him guilty and sane. He was executed on August 10, a few days after his fortieth birthday. One of his last actions was to donate his green suit to clothe the wax figure then being made of him for Madame Tussaud's Chamber of Horrors.

✳ ✳ ✳

# Shampooing Surgeon by Royal Appointment

## SAKE DEEN MAHOMED (1759-1851)

Just as fashionable, eighteenth century Brighton was coming to terms with bathing machines and hot and cold sea-water baths, a remarkable Indian therapist opened an establishment which proved so successful that it was given the accolade of appointment to the Prince of Wales. This man was Sake (another spelling for Sheikh) Deen Mahomed, who went on to become 'shampooing surgeon' to George IV. Shampooing, then, was not washing hair, but a special massaging technique used after a highly scented vapour bath. Word gradually got about that, among other things, it was an effective help to sufferers of rheumatic diseases.

After the patient had spent some time in a steam bath and was sweating freely, he was placed in a kind of small flannel tent. This had sleeves slanting inwards to allow the masseur to pummel, press and knead, while the patient could retain his modesty and avoid drafts.

Mahomed's book, *Shampooing, or Benefits Resulting from the Use of the Indian Medicated Vapour Bath,* published in Brighton in 1822, was so popular that it was republished in 1826 and again in 1838. In the book, the author claimed to be able to 'cure' asthma, paralysis, rheumatoid sciatica, lumbago, and other illnesses.

Mahomed was born at Patna, the capital of Behar in Hindustan, in India in 1759. He received a medical education in Calcutta and joined the East India Company. As a surgeon he had much early success in treating cholera which had broken out in the 27th Regiment of Native Infantry. Then, as a combatant, he served with distinction under Captain Baker, whom he had known since he was ten; Baker also became his friend. They participated in a number of skirmishes against Indian rebels. These included the storming of Gwalior, the battle of Ramnuggur and five other engagements during 1780. His colonel made Mahomed a *Soobadah* of the regiment – a local term for non-commissioned officer.

*Mahomed in court robes at the Royal Pavilion*

*Sake Deen Mahomed*

In 1784 he resigned his commission and travelled to Europe with Captain Baker's brother, also a captain. In Ireland, the former NCO went to school to perfect his English. He settled in Cork and published *The Travels of Deen Mahomed* in two volumes, which must have made him the first Indian author to write in English.

In 1786, Mahomed fell in love with a beautiful Irish girl, called Jane Daly. Here he must have come up against parental opposition for the young lovers eloped to get married. They remained in Cork for some twenty years, until about 1807.

From 1810 to about 1812, Mahomed and Jane ran a London coffee house. In order to distinguish their business from others, they emphasised its 'Indianness' and called it the Hindustanee Coffee House. However, the competition was severe and in March 1812, Mahomed declared bankruptcy. Not surprisingly, he excised all references to this London period from all future autobiographical writings.

Escaping London, Mahomed and Jane decided to try their luck in Brighton and by 1814, Mahomed was established as a bath house manager there. The couple arrived at a time of unprecedented population growth. The town was enjoying its greatest prosperity ever and the Prince of Wales (who had built his ornate seaside palace, the Royal Pavilion, in the town) was seen frequently, coming and going in his hired chaise. Many of the town's visitors were rich and spent money freely. And it was into this milieu that Mahomed introduced his new business, the first of its kind in this country. He secured premises on the sea front, close to the fashionable Steyne.

The following season was even more brilliant than the first. Everywhere, there was an atmosphere of gaiety and frivolity. Here were the kind of rich clientele with time on their hands of whom Mahomed must have dreamed.

In the beginning, however, it was still a struggle. Nobody had heard of the Indian's new methods and – in competition – warm sea-water bathing was well established. Mahomed employed a former cobbler as a very successful masseur and in an effort to break into the market, some cases were treated free. Then, after it became known that several cures had taken place – especially for rheumatic illnesses – word got around and Brighton's elite trouped to Mahomed's door.

Among his clients was the Prince of Wales, who commanded Mahomed to install one of his vapour baths in the Royal Pavilion. The Indian was given the grand-sounding appointment of Royal Shampooing Surgeon, and he remained in this royal office in the succeeding reign of William IV.

But despite this great success, there were still detractors. One such was Bernard Blackmantle who, writing in *The English Spy,* said: 'A dingy empiric has invented a new system of humbug, which is in great dispute here and is called Shampooing, a sort of stewing alive by steam, sweetened by being forced through odorous herbs, and undergoing the pleasant sensation of being stabbed all the while with pads of flannels through holes in the wet blankets that surround you until the cartilaginous substances of your joints are made as pliable as the ligaments of boiled calves' feet, your whole system relaxed and unnerved and your trembling legs as useless in supporting your body as a pair of boots would be without the usual quantity of flesh and bone within them.'

This was, however, the exception. Showers of presents poured in from grateful patients. People came from far and wide for consultation about their ailments. Amateur poets dedicated verses to Mahomed and among his illustrious clientele were Emperor Napoleon III, the Earl of Derby, the Duc de Nemoires, Lord Canning, the Marquis of Blanford, Sir Robert Peel and many, many others.

In 1830, encouraged by his success in Brighton, Mahomed opened additional premises in London, at 7 Ryder Street, St James's. By this time, his two sons had grown up and each was made responsible for one of the two businesses.

Mahomed, who retired in 1843, was long remembered as one who went out of his way to help the poor. He either gave them money or in some cases, when they were ill, offered his 'shampooing' treatment free.

He enjoyed robust good health until shortly before he died, when there was some debate about his real age. To many reckonings, he died aged 102 but to others he was ten years younger at ninety-two. He passed away at 32 Grand Parade, Brighton on February 24, 1851. His wife had pre-deceased him only two months earlier.

In the *Brighton Herald,* the obituary described Mahomed as having a constitution that was 'a stranger to disease, preserved by temperate habits and accompanied by a cheerful and contented mind, which was always conspicuous in his countenance ... He was highly respected as a man of benevolence, candour and sincerity, and in his prosperous days always had a heart and hand ready to relieve the wants of others.'

Mahomed was buried in the churchyard at St Nicholas in Brighton. The inscription on the headstone reads:

Sacred to the memory of Sake Dean [sic] Mahomed
of Patna, Hindoostan, who died on the 24th of February
1851 aged 101 years, and of Jane his wife who died on
the 26th of December 1850, aged 70 years

# To Turn a Man into a Zebra

## THE GREAT OMI (1882-1965)

He was startling to look at. From the top of his head down to his feet he was covered with zebra-like stripes. The blue-black markings curled and whirled and wiggled and twisted. Through his blue ears were sharp ivory daggers, attached to which were large ivory rings. A double-pointed ivory tusk went through his nose. His teeth had been filed to sharp points like a serpent's fangs – the lower teeth filed to fit into the top teeth. His fingernails were extravagantly long like talons, sharpened to a point and painted a brilliant red.

No wonder he was a sensation at the circus. Nor is it surprising that he was among the highest paid circus performers of his day. This was the Great Omi: in circus terms, a geek, not a freak – a freak is born like it.

The Great Omi was born plain Horace Riddler, something he always kept secret. He spent his final years near Hailsham, in Sussex, and died there in 1965.

He was born in London, the youngest son of a wealthy London land owner and his father's favourite. His early years were spent in comfort and security. His father kept horses and his groom, Joe Green, had been a clown in London. It was from Joe that Horace gained his first fascination with the world of the circus. Joe taught him the skills of a showman, and told wild, fantastic stories of the glittering life of a circus performer.

Horace was educated at a public school and decided on a career in the Army. But before he acquired his commission, his father gave him a generous allowance so that he could tour Europe and North Africa.

Wherever he went, he took pains to visit the fairgrounds, music halls and pageants. In the North African bazaars, he spent days with the acrobats, snake charmers, jugglers, and fortune tellers. He loved them all.

At the conclusion of his grand tour, Horace was commissioned into the Army as a second lieutenant. By this time, his father had

died and left him a good inheritance, but he squandered this in bad investments. Without money, he could no longer live the life of an officer and was forced to resign his commission. But with no marketable skills except those of a soldier, he tried many jobs and failed in most of them.

When war broke out in 1914, he rejoined the Army as a trooper in the cavalry. He received a second commission and was decorated for gallantry. But at the end of the war he once more joined the ranks of the unemployed. Like many other returning servicemen, he invested his modest capital in a business – in his case, a chicken farm. This failed and he lost everything.

For a while, he drifted about, both in this country and abroad but failed again to get any lasting employment. He thought of his old love of the circus and remembered from his travels that there always seemed to be work for the freaks and oddities. He would become a different kind of freak – a man tattooed from head to foot.

After an unfortunate experience with an unskilled tattooist who pretended to be Chinese, he approached a highly reputable professional called George Burchett, known as the 'King of Tattooists'. In his book, *Memoirs of a Tattooist,* Burchett describes in detail his work 'to turn a human being into a zebra'. According to Burchett, Major Riddler, as he then was, appeared as a 'tall, well-built man, with a handsome face; cultured, well spoken, and obviously of good education'.

At first Burchett refused the commission. Omi brought his own designs and explained that he wanted to be tattooed all over the body, including his face. The tattooist explained that the dies were indelible, that he would have to bear it for the rest of his life and that it was quite likely that friends and family would turn their backs on such a monster. But Horace was adamant. He realised that if he were to succeed, he would have to turn himself into something extraordinary, where there was no competition. For, above all, he wanted to be a star.

However, he had just married an attractive girl, Gladys, and knew he would have to win her over before embarking on the transformation. Happily, after a long discussion and much soul searching, she backed him all the way. Now nothing would stop him.

Burchett reluctantly agreed to do the work but insisted on obtaining the tattooing instructions in writing. It had to be an agreement by both Horace and his wife and this was done. Burchett also warned the future Great Omi that the treatment could take months, even years to complete. Horace accepted all the provisos and the work of transformation began.

Once applied to the body, the black dye changed to cobalt blue. The stripes were about one inch wide and the transformation was long, tedious and expensive. The work progressed at the rate of about two inches a day. It is said that this involved more than fifteen million needle pricks for the face and more that 500 million to cover the torso.

In addition to all this, swellings were inevitable and from time to time, the Great Omi had to spend lengthy spells in bed, on a special diet, attended by medical specialists. The total cost of all this treatment amounted to a staggering £1000 or more, a fortune in the late 1920s, which the patient had to pay from his savings. With the treatment only partly completed, he would raise money by appearances in the fairgrounds and variety shows in small towns all over the world. His wife became part of the act. Taking the name of Omette, she played the role of introducing her husband to the crowds.

As the tattooing neared completion, Horace wondered if his wife might find him ugly and unattractive. Perhaps he would be frightening to any woman. But he need not have worried. He told Burchett: 'My wife assures me it is only a matter of getting used to it, and I believe she loves me even more now than when I looked normal.'

In addition to the tattooist, he also had work done by a dentist, a vet and a plastic surgeon. The hair-bearing skin of his head and face had to be removed surgically and replaced by grafts.

But Horace was taking a terrible risk. Was he really odd enough to be employed by a circus? Had he spent all that time and money, and endured the discomfort for nothing? These were real doubts. But he needn't have had any fears. The Great Omi (in circus terms omi means 'the man') proved to be one of the really successful gambles in the world of tattooing. In 1934, almost immediately after the treatment was completed, Bertram Mills circus took him on at a substantial salary, billing him as the world's most tattooed man. Thousands queued to see him in major cities all over Europe.

In 1938, The Great Omi, accompanied by Omette, travelled to

the United States, where they joined Ripley's Believe it or Not show. They spent twenty-six weeks at the Odditorium on Broadway, toured with the Ringling Brothers-Barnum and Bailey Circus, and appeared at the Toronto Exhibition in 1940. They made two further coast-to-coast tours of the United States with seldom a spare seat in the house.

During the Second World War they became a star act in a number of shows for the RAF in Canada and played in a string of cinemas for Twentieth Century-Fox.

But as the war progressed, the Great Omi felt he must do more for his country and sailed from Halifax to Britain. On his return home, he did scores of shows for war charities and troop concerts. At the end of the war his success continued – in Manchester, London, and many other cities.

As the years went by, the Great Omi became more and more outrageous, wearing make-up and signing his pitch cards 'the Barbaric Beauty.' In one of the 1946/47 programmes of the Gigantic International Circus, he was billed as 'The Mysterious Omi – The World's Strangest Human Being – Unique, Fantastic and yet "real"'. In Manchester, he was heralded as 'the man who appears to have emanated from another world . . . mystery from the past living in the present'. And – so we're told – he is 'arrayed in beautiful sequinned gold velvet robes, woven specially in the Lyon mills of France'.

Towards the end of his life, in the mid-1950s, Omi and his wife retired to a mobile home on the Deanland Wood site at Golden Cross, in Sussex. The showman was a regular shopper in Hailsham High Street. One has to speculate as to how other shoppers reacted to this 'free show'. But in a report in the *Sussex Express* in 1984, a local shopkeeper, Reg Searle, was quoted as saying: 'He was a nice bloke. He was well educated and acted quite normally. But he had to be seen to be believed . . . he livened up our lives . . . I was sorry when he disappeared or died.'

But who knows the mind of an ex-zebra on retirement? According to *Art, Sex and Symbol,* by RWB Scuff and Christopher Gotch, the Great Omi suffered a mental breakdown towards the end of his life. He died in 1965, at the age of eighty-three. After a quiet funeral, he was buried in Chalvington churchyard.

✳ ✳ ✳

# The Man Who Wasn't There
## PILTDOWN MAN (1913-1953)

The Piltdown affair wasn't just one of the world's greatest hoaxes. It was also one of the century's most puzzling whodunits. In the years proceeding the First World War, near the Sussex village of Piltdown, someone secreted in the ground specially doctored, apparently human remains. Once discovered, the find was hailed by almost the entire scientific community as representing the ancient 'missing link' between ape and man.

Four decades later, in 1953, the supposed missing link was re-examined, treated with modern dating methods, and found to be a hoax. But who was the perpetrator? And why did he or she do it? Over the years the finger has been pointed at a number of people, now all dead, but no final conclusion has been reached to suit everyone.

In 1908, a workman digging in a shallow gravel pit outside Barkham Manor near Piltdown, found what was at first thought to be a coconut. The workman broke it up but one piece was kept to show to Charles Dawson, a lawyer managing the estate and an accomplished amateur archaeologist. Dawson, who lived at Castle Lodge, Lewes, identified the find as part of an exceptionally thick human skull.

Suspecting that the workman had discovered something important, Dawson repeatedly visited first the original site (termed Piltdown I) and later two further sites in the vicinity (Piltdown II and III). The first fragment to come into his hands was the left parietal bone. Then, in the autumn of 1911, he discovered part of the left temporal bone which fitted onto the original find. There were more finds, some belonging to the skull but also a fossil hippopotamus tooth.

In the spring of 1912 Dawson took all his finds to the British Museum (Natural History), now the Natural History Museum, and showed them to Dr Smith Woodward, Keeper of Geology. Woodward was an old acquaintance to whom Dawson had brought previous discoveries. Sensing that Dawson may have been on to something important, Woodward arranged to accompany him to the gravel pit in May 1912.

After further digging, Dawson found the left half of a jaw-bone (mandible). He continued to work throughout that summer, during which time a number of further finds were revealed. These comprised eight pieces of a human cranium, the jaw bone, some nine or ten fragments of mammalian teeth and bones, and some rough flint implements.

On December 18, 1912, Dawson and Woodward addressed a meeting of the Geological Society of London. They outlined their sensational discoveries and Piltdown Man was christened *Eoanthropus dawsoni,* Dawson's Dawn Man. To many British anthropologists, this was the specimen they had been waiting for, ever since Darwin's theories of evolution had been published in 1859. This at last was the Missing Link, that had been so long sought, a being that was neither ape nor man but a development in between.

In the days before carbon dating and other modern methods, scientists at the British Museum dated Piltdown Man older than the Neanderthals and Cro-Magnons found on continental Europe. This could mean one thing: the first man must have been a British native. The bones were thought to come from Pliocene deposits (roughly two million years old). A buzz went around the academic world and dozens of papers were issued giving varying views on Piltdown Man and how he fitted in with our evolutionary history.

But a few voices, mainly from the United States, did express concern. In 1914, William Gregory, a palaeontologist at the American Museum of Natural History in New York, noted the following: 'It has been suspected by some that geologically (the bones) are not that old at all; that they even represent a deliberate hoax, a Negro or Australian skull and a broken ape jaw, artificially fossilised and planted in the grave bed to fool scientists.'

The controversy raged for the next four decades; most scientists and the general public accepted the Piltdown Man as a fact. Then in 1953 Kenneth Oakley, a palaeontologist at the British Museum, and Joseph S Weiner and Wilfred Le Gros Clark, both anatomists at Oxford, re-examined the bones and found unequivocal indications of forgery. The lower jaw appeared to come from a young female orang-utan and the teeth had been filed flat to appear more human.

*The Piltdown Men – front row, AS Underwood, Arthur Keith, WP Pycraft, Ray Lankester: back row, RO Barlow, Grafton Elliot Smith, Charles Dawson, Arthur Smith Woodward. From a painting by John Cooke*

There were a number of other indications. For example, the hinge of the jaw had been broken to prevent anybody discovering that it didn't fit the human skull. The chin of the jaw, which would have showed its simian origins, was missing.

It became apparent that all the bones had been soaked in a solution of potassium dichromate. This not only hardened the remains, it produced a patina, apparently a result of great age. The skull may also have been boiled in an iron sulphate solution. The hoaxer had done his work well.

But who was the hoaxer and why did he do it? There have been scores of articles and a run of books, putting different men into the dock. In 1983, John Winslow, an American anthropologist, published an article in *Science 83,* implicating Crowborough resident, Sir Arthur Conan Doyle. It was the name arrived at after Winslow had spent an amazing 2,000 hours of sleuthing.

But why had nobody else been on Doyle's trail? After all, scientists from all over the world had produced many theories and just as many perpetrators. Winslow added this caveat: 'That Doyle had not been implicated in the hoax before now not only is a testament to the skill with which he appears to have perpetrated it, but it also explains why the case against him is circumstantial, intricate, even convoluted. For to be on his trail is, in a sense, to be on the trail of the world's greatest fictional detective himself, Sherlock Holmes.' After all, if he was able to engineer so many intricate and convoluted fictional cases, surely he was capable of dreaming up such a hoax as the Piltdown Man.

But Conan Doyle was only one suspect among several. In 1955, Weiner published *The Piltdown Forgery,* in which he named Dawson as the guilty man. According to Weiner, Dawson wanted something spectacular to enable him to join the Royal Society.

But Ronald Millar, in *The Piltdown Men,* argued that Dawson, who died in 1916, was too obvious a suspect. He wrote: 'I find it impossible to believe that Dawson would pit his meagre knowledge of anatomy (if it is accepted that he had any at all) against that of any skilled anatomist . . .The threat of exposure would be too perpetual.'

Why then was the hoax so very successful? In Richard Harter's paper on the internet, he gives several main reasons: a) the team finding the specimens (Dawson, Woodward) had excellent credentials; b) incompetence on the part of the British Palaeontological community; c) the relatively primitive analytical tools available circa 1920; d) skill of the forgery; e) it matched what was expected from theory'; and f) as Millar remarks, "the hoax led a charmed life".

Woodward has also been named, both as the perpetrator and victim. It was suggested that somebody wanted to make Woodward look ridiculous after the hoax was exposed.

But one of the most recent candidates has been Martin Hinton, a curator of zoology at the Natural History Museum at the time of the hoax. In 1976, Hinton's trunk was discovered under the roof of the museum. The contents included a number of bones stained and carved in the same way as the Piltdown Man fossils and other artefacts. When analysed, it was found that the bones were enriched in iron and magnesium in the same proportions as in Piltdown Man.

Hinton's choice of Sussex could be easily explained. He knew the area well including the knowledge that the Piltdown gravels were entirely without fossils. He could thus seed the area wherever he saw fit.

Hinton knew that Dawson was very much the amateur and should be easily fooled. Dawson had already unknowingly traded a stone implement, stained by Hinton to look old, with Harry Morris. When this turned up later, it was labelled that it had been fraudulently stained by Dawson.

If Hinton were the hoaxer, what was his motive? An explanation given in *Nature* concerns Woodward and an argument over money. In 1910, Hinton wrote to Woodward asking if he could catalogue rodent remains at the museum during his holiday but also asking to be paid for the work. What happened is not known, but for the rest of his career Hinton kept well away from Woodward's palaeontology department, despite the fact that he generally specialised in this work.

Professor Brian Gardiner, professor of palaeontology at King's College, London, is convinced that Hinton was the sole hoaxer. He points out that Hinton was well known for his practical jokes and that the Piltdown forgery would have been a good way to get back at a pompous, stuffy keeper of palaeontology.

However, Richard Harter points out that the case against Hinton is full of flaws. The quarrel about money took place in 1911; the first finds were in 1908. The chemical analyses do not match. Hinton doctored bones with, amongst other things, manganese. The Piltdown finds do not contain manganese. Hinton's samples do not contain gypsum; the Piltdown samples do. And most importantly, Hinton did not have the necessary access to the site in the 1912-1914 period.

Who really was the hoaxer? The simple fact is that we do not know. No theory stands out that can't be faulted. So, despite the periodic and enthusiastic claims, the truth is that we'll probably never know for sure. All the suspects are long dead. And nobody yet has managed to obtain information from beyond the grave.

# 'A Pervert - and the Most Charming of Men'

## COUNT ERIC STENBOCK (1860-1895)

Contemporaries had many strange things to say about Count Stanislaus Eric Magnus Andreas Harry Stenbock whose family house, Withdeane Hall, is in Patcham, Brighton. He was known as a 'scholar, connoisseur and drunkard,' and described as 'decadent, bizarre, fantastic, feverish, eccentric, extravagant, morbid, and perverse'. He was a writer of prose and poetry and his work was criticised as 'an elaborate and screaming parody ... of the youthful decadent, the affected precariousness, the sham mysticism, the sham aestheticism ... the ridiculous medley of Neo-Paganism and Neo-Catholicism.'

Eric Stenbock lived in a haze of opium smoke and incense with a pet toad called Fatima. Around his neck a snake coiled like a scarf. Eric kept other animals in his room such as lizards and salamanders and in his garden was what he described as his 'zoo' – three reindeer, a bear and a fox.

He also appears to have kept a shrine both in Estonia, where he came from, and a smaller version in his house in Sloane Terrace, Chelsea. He had a statue of Buddha, a bust of Shelley, a statue of Eros and other gods. Two red votive lamps were kept burning continuously. Once when Oscar Wilde was visiting, the playwright committed the sacrilege of lighting his cigarette from the shrine lamp. Eric fell to the floor in a real or a histrionic swoon. Wilde, completely unconcerned, stepped over the body of his host, took two or three puffs of his cigarette, and left the house.

Eric had Swedish, Russian and Scottish blood and was heir to vast estates in Estonia, owned by his family since the eighteenth century. He also owned a castle in a remote region of Russia. However, he was born in Cheltenham, where his family lived at Thirlestaine Hall until they moved to Brighton in 1874, when Eric was about fourteen. His father was Eric Stenbock, Count de Bogesund, Baron de Torpa, his mother, Lucy Sophia Fredrichs of

Thirlestaine Hall.

Eric's father died when his son and heir was still young. His mother married again, to Frank Mowatt, a shy and good humoured man, and had three sons and three daughters from this marriage. Mowatt should have been a good step-father but Eric hated him. He was, however, happy to accompany Mowatt to visit Queen Victoria. The Queen apparently found Eric good company as, after this, it was said she often sent for him.

But it wasn't just the Queen who was taken with Eric Stenbock. He so impressed himself upon his contemporaries that they wrote of him in various memoirs and anecdotes that far outstrip the attention given to his prose and

*Count Eric Stenbock*

poetry. He became acquainted with many of the key figures of the day – Beardsley, Yeats, Symons and Lionel Johnson – and they remembered him in their writings with great affection.

In his 1940 biography, Ernest Rhys, who won fame as editor of the Everyman books, described his first sight of Stenbock. 'The maid announced him and he looked most unusual: very fair hair beautifully curled, and a round, blue-eyed face, with yellow eyebrows. He was short and slightly built. He waved his head as he paused at the door, and took a little gold phial out of his pocket, from which he anointed his fingers before passing them through his locks. He was like a magnified child; and it took me a moment to believe he could be real.'

Rhys continued: 'He sat down by me, drunk off a cup of tea impetuously, asked me if I liked Russian music, and next moment seated himself at the piano and fell to improvising. He played variations, apparently his own, upon a Ukrainian melody and put us all under his spell – I had heard nothing like it before.'

Eric was educated abroad and then spent four terms at Balliol College, Oxford, from 1879. He didn't stay for a degree. It was said that at university he and his friends tried a new religion every week. Eric wrote love poems addressed to various young men, several to a Berkshire youth, Charles Bertram Fowler, who died of consumption at the age of sixteen. The poet also wrote stories about witches, demons and werewolves based on folk tales of his native land.

As a writer, his output was sparse. There were two slim volumes of poems. *Love, Sleep and Dreams* was published circa 1881 and *Myrtle, Rue and Cypress* in 1883. However, some critics feel his tales of the supernatural were among his best writing and regret that he has left us only one volume of such work.

In 1885, Stenbock inherited his ancestral domain and seems to have spent most of the next year or so visiting his estate. However, from 1886 to 1890, he lived at 11 Sloane Terrace, London SW1, and at 21 Gloucester Walk, London W8, from 1890.

In 1891, Eric fell madly in love with the young theatrical composer, Norman O'Neill, whom he met on the top of a Piccadilly bus. Some two years later, when O'Neill became a student of the Hoch Conservatory in Frankfurt, Stenbock took a great interest in his progress, and sent him a series of humorous sketches by Aubrey Beardsley. Eric also remembered O'Neill in his will, enabling the student to stay on for a valuable further year.

By 1895, Eric's addiction to drugs and alcohol had reduced him to a state where he could no longer look after himself and he was taken to his mother's home in Brighton. His fine chiselled features coarsened and his once proud head of hair began to drop out. For his diet, he could manage little more than bread and milk.

But even before this, he had become increasingly obsessed with death. His last collection of poems, *The Shadow of Death,* which came out in 1893, contains many haunting, bitter-sweet evocations of the poet's past life and his anticipation of its end. *Studies of Death: Romantic Tales,* published in 1894, included *The Egg of the Albatross,* which Stenbock-expert John Adlard regards as his best.

Other tales include *Hylas, Narcissus,* and the fine, subtle *The True Story of a Vampire.*

Towards the end of his life, Eric became mentally as well as physically ill. At Withdeane Hall, he terrified the domestic staff with his persecution complex. His delirious tremors so frightened the Mowatt children that they moved to distant rooms in the house.

On his previous travels, Eric had been accompanied by a dog, a monkey and a life-size doll. He was now convinced that the doll was his son and he referred to it as 'le petit comte'. Every day, it had to be brought to him and when the doll was not there, Eric would ask for news of its health. There was even the rumour that a dishonest monk or Jesuit had exhorted large sums of money from Eric under the pretence of paying for the education of the doll.

Finally, on April 26, 1895, in a drunken rage, Eric attacked someone with a poker. Losing his balance, he hit his head on the stone fireplace and this killed him. His heart was cut out and sent to Estonia, where it was preserved in a wall in the church at Kusal. The rest of Eric Stenbock was buried in Brighton's Extra-Mural Cemetery in Lewes Road. It was the first day of the trial of his friend, Oscar Wilde, charged with homosexuality. Eric was just thirty-six years of age.

At the time of his death, in far away Estonia, something mystical occurred. Eric's uncle and heir was working late into the night as a storm raged outside. Thinking he heard somebody call, he put down his pen. He was suddenly engulfed with inconsolable grief and turning towards the rain-lashed window, he saw Eric's tear-stained face staring in at him. The next day a telegram came informing him of Eric's death. He was convinced that death had occurred at the same moment as he had seen the vision.

Withdeane Hall still stands. After the Mowatts left it was used as a preparatory school for boys and a billet for troops during World War Two before being converted into flats in 1950. Its extensive grounds were developed as Varndean Gardens and Withdean Crescent.

# A Rare Glimpse of an 18th Century Village

## THOMAS TURNER (1729-1792)

**B**etween 1745 and 1756, in East Hoathly, the village shopkeeper, Thomas Turner, kept a diary recording the minutiae of daily life – about himself, his family and his fellow citizens. Turner occupied a key position in the small community where he was grocer, mercer, draper, undertaker, schoolmaster, surveyor, tax-gatherer, writer of wills and accounts, distributor of charity, churchwarden, overseer of the poor and much else.

A diary is perhaps the truest account of people and events and succeeds in a way impossible by any other means. The author of an autobiography may select and edit the things he remembers or thinks he remembers. A diarist sets down events as they happen.

Turner was an honest man with few pretensions and, even though much of the diary is boringly repetitive, we feel it has the ring of truth. This is what mid-eighteenth century East Hoathly was really like.

Thomas Turner was born in Groombridge on June 9, 1729, the son of a yeoman, John Turner. His mother, a girl from Rotherfield, was his father's second wife. When Thomas was not quite six, the family moved to Framfield, where his father bought a shop. We know nothing of Thomas's education but it is thought he probably went to school in Lewes. Here he would have learned to write in the clear hand of the diary and to do the sums and accounting for the village.

Around 1751 he set up his shop in East Hoathly, some three miles from his parents' house in Framfield. The diarist had a large brick house, part of which was the shop. It is now three cottages, located in the High Street. Most things which came into the village would have passed through Turner's shop. He dealt direct from the supplier – cloth from the weavers, nails from the blacksmith, salt from the fishermen and flour from the millers. Some goods were delivered, others he would have fetched himself.

*Thomas Turner's house in East Hoathly*

He was also a purchasing agent for the entire village and spent much time obtaining customers' specific orders – from East Hoathly, Lewes or further afield. He even did his share of barbering, when a man wanted a better cut than he'd get from his wife. He turned hair into wigs which he then sold on. He ran his business on very long-term credit and it is likely that he earned no more than around £60 annually. His son, however, was reputed to have made from £50,000 to £70,000 a year from the same shop, forty years on.

The diary isn't about the great and famous. Turner is much more concerned with the likes of Elizabeth Ellis, made pregnant by the village rogue and later found dead in suspicious circumstances. The next time a local girl becomes pregnant he acts in his capacity as a vestry official and is determined to find the father so that the girl does not become a charge on parish funds.

Day by day we read of the health of Turner's wife, of the earning and spending of personal and parish funds, even what was for dinner. The basic diet of most villagers would have been bread, potatoes and turnips, with greens in season. Occasional meat for most people would often have been the innards of an animal rather than the flesh and the commonest method of preparation was boiling the food in a bag. Good hygiene was unknown and in one entry Turner remarks that he and some friends sat down to a meal of lamb's pluck which the cat had been picking at earlier. Few, even the wealthy, would have eaten any kind of meat out of season. Root feeding of animals was not practised during the winter and the butcher would slaughter only from spring to autumn.

When the diary begins Turner was twenty-four and recently married to Margaret Slater, whom he called Peggy. She was the twenty-year-old daughter of a Hartfield farming couple. Five months into the marriage Peggy became pregnant and gave birth to a boy who lived for only five months. Early on it became apparent that the marriage was not a success; Turner described his wife as a capricious, complaining and sickly woman. Throughout their first seven years together the diary records Turner's increasing unhappiness. Visits from medical men to his wife became so frequent that there were rumours of Turner hastening her death by conniving at a savage gynaeocological operation. Peggy died on June 23, 1761, following a long drawn out and painful illness, believed to be a disease of the bladder and reproductive organs, for which there was then no cure. In the mid-eighteenth century a frequent panacea for most illnesses was to bleed the patient and much bleeding was resorted to with Peggy.

It is interesting to note the diarist's attitude to his wife before and after her death. Here is an entry for Friday, October 15, 1756, on their third wedding anniversary:

> Doubtless many have been the disputes which have happened between my wife and myself during the time, and many have been the afflictions which it has pleased God to lay upon us, and which we have justly deserved by the many animosities and dissension which have been almost incessantly continued and fermented between us and our friends from almost the first day of our marriage.

There was an abrupt change following his wife's death. Thomas began to feel lonely and imagined his marriage as it might have been. The following entry was written on the day of her death, but he expressed such sentiments for some considerable time:

> I have lost a sincere friend and virtuous wife, a prudent and good economist in family and a very

valuable companion.

He was sufficiently depressed to suppose there was a serious loss of trade, but the reality was somewhat different. By 1766 things had gone so well that Turner was able to buy his shop. He also bought the best pub in the village and several parcels of land in the district.

Much life in the village was convivial. We read about the unexpected windfalls when confiscated brandy was taken from smugglers by the excise men and shared among the villagers. Feasts and boisterous parties were enjoyed, after one of which the rector's wife helped drag Turner from his bed in the early hours and make him dance, dressed in his wife's petticoat. There were also cock fights, cricket matches, horse racing, betting and long drinking sessions.

Drink was one of Turner's problems. He was both a deeply religious man and a drunkard and a lot of writing is taken up trying to reconcile the two. Typical is the entry for Thursday, October 21, 1756:

> I must, I believe, drink nothing but water, for I
> find a glass or two of liquor makes me drunk, for
> today I could not get home sober.

The next day he commiserated:

> Oh cruel is my misfortune (that I cannot bear the
> least matter of liquor).

He was ever ready to enlist the help of God. This is the entry for Friday, October 8, 1756:

> Daily and hourly do I sin ... and may the God of
> all goodness pour into my heart his holy spirit.

Historians have known of Turner's diaries for about 150 years, since RW Blencowe and MA Lower published extracts in the *Sussex Archaeological Collections* in 1859. This, however, did little justice to Turner. Diary extracts were, in many cases, mistranscribed and often wrongly aligned chronologically. In 1948 Dean K Worcester's excellent *The Life and Times of Thomas Turner of East Hoathly* was published, and in 1984 David Vaisey, then Keeper of Western Manuscripts at the Bodlaian Library, Oxford, and Fellow of Exeter College, went back to Turner's original manuscript. He reduced the 330,000 plus words to around 130,000 and published the diaries in one manageable volume – *The Diary of Thomas Turner 1754-1765*. The entries left out were, mainly, Turner's moralising, many pages of figures and much repetition.

The diary ends on July 31, 1765, with Turner's second marriage to Mary (he called her Molly) Hicks of Chiddingly, a servant to one of the Justices of the Peace. Perhaps it was an indication of the shopkeeper's new found happiness that he ended the diary here. This happiness must have been a bonus for, in the mid-eighteenth century, few had the privilege to marry for love. Turner would have looked for a companion able to do the work in the house and give him children.

They had seven children, two of whom died in infancy. Two of the boys followed family tradition and became mercers. Turner lived for a quarter of a century after finishing his diary. He died on February 11, 1793, aged sixty-three. Molly survived him by fourteen years.

Turner did not record great national events, nor was it his intention to be an historian. His was a small world peopled on the whole by ordinary people. Nevertheless, he gave a rare, localised view of life in a Georgian village. From his own point of view, the purpose of his diary was to make sure he remembered his actions and kept his books straight. That was what he set out to do, and he did it well.

# The Man who Created Pooh

## Alan Alexander Milne (1882-1956)

For children of all ages, in many parts of the world, some of their favourite story-time characters have come alive to them through the genius of one man. This is the author AA Milne, of Cotchford Farm on Ashdown Forest. In collaboration with illustrator Ernest Shepard he produced some of the most popular children's stories ever published – the Pooh books.

But just as Arthur Conan Doyle wanted to be known for stories other than those devoted to Sherlock Holmes, so Milne yearned to be recognised for his plays and novels, and not just for *Winnie the Pooh*. After all, it was no mean feat, aged twenty-four in 1906, to be appointed Assitant Editor of *Punch* or, several years later, to be picking up more than £1,000 a year as a Fleet Street freelance. He published a number of essays and papers, mainly in *Punch,* which show a lively wit and a fluent pen. He subsequently enjoyed great success both as a playright and novelist.

Alan Alexander Milne was born on January 18, 1882, at Henley House School in Kilburn. He was the youngest of three sons. His father, John Vine Milne, was a Scotsman who had married Sarah Maria, daughter of a manufacturer. Both parents were teachers at private schools. At one of these, Henley School, HG Wells was a science teacher and he became a close family friend.

The young Milne won a scholarship to Westminster School at the age of eleven, an unprecedented achievement, and later proceeded to Trinity College, Cambridge. He disappointed his tutor by accepting the editorship of the student magazine *Granta,* and preferring journalism to mathematics in which, in 1903, he achieved only a third. His father was so angry that he refused to speak to his son for a week. But Alan was determined to be a writer and not just to write but to write precisely what interested him.

In 1913 he married Dorothy, daughter of Martin de Selincourt, a city merchant, and god-daughter of the editor of *Punch.* As part of the settlement Dorothy took one of her parents' many servants to act as her personal maid. Together with a cook, they all moved into a splendid flat in Chelsea.

Milne's writing was interrupted by the 1914-18 war with Germany. He joined the Royal Warwickshire Regiment in 1915 and was sent for military training to the Isle of Wight, where he was joined by his wife. It was said they had the prettiest cottage in Sandown, and it was here that he wrote his first novel, *Once on a Time,* a children's story.

With the help of a friend Milne was soon commissioned into the armed services and found the experience of warfare not uncongenial. However, on the Somme, he caught trench fever and was sent back to the Isle of Wight to convalesce. There he wrote several plays, some produced during wartime. Of the war he wrote: 'I was a pacifist before 1914 but this (I thought with other fools) was a war to end all wars.' He was transferred to Intelligence and finished the war writing propaganda in the War Office.

After he was demobbed, Milne found his old desk at *Punch* occupied. He was asked to write occasional pieces but found this humiliating, and decided instead to concentrate on writing for the theatre.

His first work was a short play, *Werzel Flummery,* slight and whimsical. By 1919 he had completed five plays, in all of which could be seen the influence of JM Barrie. Critics praised his ready wit, good humour and the way he sustained a range of illusion and genuine dramatic effect. Then in 1920 *Mr Pim Passes By* was produced to thunderous applause, his most successful play to date. More plays followed, making Milne one of the most popular playwrights of his generation. Perhaps the most interesting and long-lived was *Toad of Toad Hall,* an adaptation of Kenneth Grahame's *The Wind in The Willows.*

In 1920 the Milne family was surprised by the birth of a son. He was called Christopher Robin and Milne's life was to be changed forever.

On a wet day in Wales he began writing a children's book of verse. *When We Were Very Young* appeared in 1924 and was an immediate success. The following year Milne bought Cotchford Farm on the edge of Ashdown Forest. From then on weekends and holidays were spent in Sussex, the family driving down from Chelsea in the blue Fiat with Christopher Robin on his nanny's lap.

Milne wanted to write more children's stories and Dorothy had

the idea of turning their son's soft toys into active animals having adventures with Christopher Robin. Critics have seen similarities between the toy characters and friends and relations of Milne. Like all writers of fiction, he borrowed bits of personalities from those around him. Richard Adams, for example, has suggested that Eeyore is 'the first portrait in English literature of a type of neurotic we all know too well'. And the reason Eeyore was such a miserable little animal? The toy had lost some of its neck stuffing and its head drooped sadly.

*Winnie the Pooh* came out in 1926, *Now We Are Six* in 1927 and *The House at Pooh Corner* in 1928, and all were tremendous successes. The illustrator, who is almost equally responsible for the books' popularity, was Ernest Shepard. Milne was not immediately taken with the artist but nevertheless gave him very detailed instructions – more detailed than Shepard had had from any other author. Milne was anxious for Shepard to 'meet' Pooh and the other animal-toys and the artist made a special trip to Milne's Sussex house. This was important for Shepard, too, as he always drew from models. It was not until after Milne's death in 1956 that Shepard admitted using his own son, Grahame, as the model for Christopher Robin. The real Christopher Robin, he said, had legs that were 'too skinny'.

Shepard followed the author's writing to the letter. The author and his illustrator strolled about Ashdown Forest, Milne pointing out the real sites that feature in the stories. You can still see most of them today, despite the devastation made by the 1987 hurricane. There is Gills Lap, 'the enchanted place on the very top of the Forest'; there is the same bridge on which the friends played Poohsticks; and there, just as Pooh and Christopher Robin had seen it, is 'the whole world spread out until it reached the sky'.

Strangely, Milne admitted that he was not inordinately fond of children, or even interested in them. His own son, Christopher, saw little of his parents. His mother might amuse herself with the child for the odd half-hour, and Milne did his best to keep his son entertained, but it was laboured and neither father nor son were comfortable. Perhaps the father looked for companionship with the child and, not finding it, discovered a substitute in the make-believe world of fiction. Years later, as an adult, Christopher

*Pooh Bridge*

Robin wrote: 'I might not have missed my mother had she disappeared, and would certainly not have missed my father. I would have missed Nanny – most desolately.'

In 1929 Christopher Robin went to boarding school, his nanny left to be married and the Pooh books came to an end. The Shepard-Milne partnership had brought fame to both men and made Christopher Robin and Pooh household names around the world. The books were widely translated, including into Japanese and Bulgarian. But to Milne, enough was enough and he wanted to do other writing, not involving children.

AA Milne's autobiography, *It's Too Late Now,* came out to good reviews just three weeks before the Second World War began in 1939. Throughout hostilities, he wrote frequently to *The Times* on the state of the war and other matters. When *Chloe Marr* was published in 1946 it was his first novel for thirteen years, and it would be his last. The book was a significant success, both in Britain and America. One critic wrote: 'The Old Enchanter has done it again.'

Christopher Milne survived active service in the war and married in 1948. He had always been embarrassed by his fame as Christopher Robin, but wrote three books and a collection of memoirs about his early life.

AA Milne died on January 31, 1956. He was seventy-four. He had once written that everyone seeks immortality, a name left behind him that will live forever. In the characters of Pooh and his friends, perhaps Milne achieved just that.

✳ ✳ ✳

# 15,000 Feet and Rising

## DOLLY SHEPHERD (1886-1983)

**D**olly Shepherd stepped into the record books on June 8, 1908, above Ashby-de-la-Zouch in Leicestershire, with the first-ever mid-air rescue. Dolly was an experienced aeronaut, quite used to putting on a show for the crowds. On this particular day she was billed to make a double descent with Louie May, a novice parachutist making her first jump. They would both go up together, sitting on the side of the basket attached to the Mammoth, the largest balloon in the country. Then they would jump at the same time, each with her own parachute.

That was the plan. However, a sudden shower before take-off damaged the Mammoth, deflated it and set its 108,000 cubic feet of dangerous gas spilling among the crowd. There was panic as everyone put distance between themselves and the gas, to frantic cries of 'No smoking! Gas escaping!'

Not wanting to disappoint the huge crowd, Dolly agreed that both she and Louie would make an ascent attached to her smaller solo balloon of 20,000 cubic feet capacity.

In those days there was no pack, not even a harness. The parachutist was suspended beneath the parachute, merely holding on to a trapeze bar, with a sling (a six-inch wide piece of webbing) between the legs to help take the weight of the body. The apex of the parachute was attached directly beneath the balloon when going solo, or to the underside of the basket of a right-away, or manned, balloon – the captain, or pilot, taking three or four fee-paying passengers and landing some five miles away.

Balloons were filled either with 'hot-air' or gas. The former was used only when gas was not available, as inflation was tedious, entailing the digging of a finally covered fire trench and the use of a pulley to haul the balloon, made of a special heavy rubberised material, over a chimney to receive the hot air, or smoke, from the fire trench. Disadvantages were that the balloon would have to ascend immediately, and the parachutist would have to 'pull away' to descend at about 1,500 feet, as by then the air would start to cool, and the balloon to deflate.

Gas-filled balloons were quicker and easier to inflate. A long pipe was attached to the neck of the balloon, and the other end to an ordinary domestic gas point. By this method the balloon could remain in situ as long as required, and the parachutist could go as high as he or she wished. Dolly usually went to 4-5,000 feet.

On this fateful day in June 1908 the ascent under Dolly's small solo balloon went well as it rose with its unusually heavy load, and they reached 3,000 feet, ready for the descent. Louie pulled the liberating cord that gave her independent support from her own parachute. Nothing happened. She pulled it again with the same result. Again and again. And all the time the balloon continued to rise. At 8,000 feet, still rising, they passed through clouds into sunlight. Below them the earth had disappeared from view and it was much, much colder. Dolly saw that Louie's face was deathly white, her lips blue with cold, her eyes wide open and staring with suppressed fear. When Dolly's aneroid showed 11,000 feet she took the only decision possible. They would both descend on one parachute – Dolly's. It would be a terrible risk. The drop would be much too fast. But the alternative was certain death.

Following Dolly's instructions, Louie mechanically transferred herself on to Dolly's body, wrapping her legs around Dolly's waist and her arms around her neck. One slip

*Dolly in the earliest of her three daring knickerbocker suits*

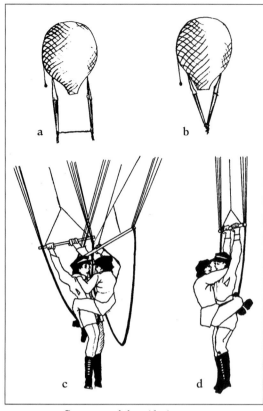

*Sequences of the mid-air rescue:*
*a, Ascent under individual parachutes; b, Getting*
*together; c, The transfer; d, Descent*

and there were two miles of nothingness between them and the ground. Holding them both with one hand, Dolly pulled the ripping cord and the terrifying descent began.

Together they hurtled downwards, the earth seeming to come head-on towards them like an express train out of control. Just missing a razor-sharp upturned scythe, and six feet from a road, they smashed into a field. Miraculously Louie was unhurt but Dolly suffered damage to the pelvis and spinal paralysis. She was told she would not walk again, but thanks to a primitive form of 'electrical' treatment given by a local doctor, she was back in the air two months later and survived other aerial adventures.

Dolly, who spent the last twenty years of her long life in Eastbourne, was born on November 19, 1886, in Potters Bar, the daughter of a London policeman. She was christened Elizabeth Mariam, but was called Dolly from the time she was a small child. She had an older brother, David, and a younger sister, Wene.

On a spring day in 1903, when Dolly was sixteen, she travelled to Alexandra Palace in London, where she was to take up her appointment with destiny. She had always admired the great American march king, John Philip Sousa, and she had learned he was to give two performances there – but the tickets had sold out. Nothing daunted, Dolly applied for and got a job as a waitress in the

Great Hall where Sousa was to perform. During the interval Sousa came to one of her tables, with Captain Auguste Gaudron, a celebrated French balloonist and parachutist, and an American showman, Samuel Franklin Cody (nicknamed the Colonel). After Sousa's departure the two other men continued to go to one of Dolly's tables and the hovering waitress felt drawn to their conversation. They spoke of balloons and parachutes and heavier-than-air machines – this before the Wright brothers had made their initial 852 foot hop.

The Colonel was putting on shows at the Bijou Theatre, attached to Alexandra Palace, and one of his stunts was to shoot an egg from his wife's head. One evening he grazed her scalp so that part of the act would have to be cancelled. Dolly felt so sorry for him that she burst out, to the startled men: 'I'll do it for you. I'll come tonight!' And she was as good as her word.

In gratitude, the Colonel took Dolly round the aeronautical workshop set up in the old banqueting hall. Wide-eyed with excitement, Dolly marvelled at the kites, the deflated balloons, parachutes, wicker baskets and other paraphernalia used in flying. Sensing her excitement, Captain Gaudron asked Dolly if *she* would like to make a parachute descent. The answer was an unequivocal yes.

It was a year before Captain Gaudron wrote, inviting her to make her first jump. But before it took place she had to undergo the necessary training – all thirty minutes of it. She learned the basic requirements of a parachutist were strong arms and wrists, and she was shown how to hold on to a trapeze bar, stand astride the 'sling' and how to fall.

Dolly never forgot her first jump. She was accompanied in the basket of a right-away balloon ascent by Captain Gaudron and three fee-paying passengers. When they reached 2,000 feet she heard his voice advising her to get ready. Later, Dolly wrote: 'It was like a piece of ice dropped into the pit of my stomach. Oh, that first fall! What a heady mixture of fright and sheer exhilaration! My heart rose into my mouth as I plummeted for what seemed far too long, dropping like a stone. I could hear the rapid flap-flap-flap of the silk streaming after me as the canopy broke from the balloon netting and sucked at the rush of air, and then at last there was a big whooooooosh . . . the sling tightened and the trapeze bar tugged at my arms; the parachute was open.'

How she loved it all! At seventeen Dolly was ready for the life of a parachutist. She joined the Captain's team at Alexandra Palace, and performed in London, Scotland, Wales and the Midlands, at £2.10s each ascent.

Dolly became a celebrity. She learned to love the adulation of the crowds and the VIP treatment. She visited factories, went down a coal mine, drove a train, had tea with groups of miners' wives and dined with Sir Robert Peel, a descendent of the famous Prime Minister of the same name.

But there were still real risks. On one occasion, alone at 12,000 feet, she was unable to detach herself from the balloon, which continued upwards through the clouds. It reached 15,000 feet, still rising. The air was icily cold and night fell. Dolly knew she had to wait until sufficient gas had seeped out for the baloon to descend. Grimly, she hung on to the trapeze bar with one hand while she bit the fingers of the other in an effort to get the blood circulating.

*Dolly ascending above Alexandra Palace*

After three long hours, Dolly, at times semi-conscious, finally descended on to a field at midnight. Half-frozen and desperately tired, she made her way to the small station at Whissendine in Rutland, from where a telegram was sent to the Captain.

In those days, ballooning and parachuting were spectator entertainments only, carried out by only a few groups of men and women usually at galas and fêtes. Dolly took the spills along with the thrills. She never knew where she might land – on a roof top, in trees, pulled through bushes or blown backwards on to a barbed wire fence. On one occasion she seemed about to fall in front of an express train, when quick thinking by the train driver saved the day as he let off steam. The force of the steam simply blew her away. At another time the parachute cords broke and she fell back on to the crowd. At yet another, after a long drop, her parachute didn't open until she was at tree height.

By 1910 aeroplanes were beginning to take over from balloons. As a professional aeronaut, Dolly was able to meet and mix with the new flying fraternity. Those involved with both planes and balloons began to see the parachute not just as a

*Dolly prepares for take-off*

form of entertainment but as a life-saver. Trials began that eventually saw the production of the parachute harness.

Then, on a fine spring evening in 1912, as Dolly was swaying gently, high above Alexandra Palace, a clear voice reached her out of the ether: 'Don't come up again,' it said, 'or you will be killed.' She looked around her for the voice – there was nothing but empty sky. 'All right,' she replied aloud. Back on the ground she gave away the Union Jack (which was waved to the crowd as she went up, then tucked into her clothing), her cap and her badges, and told the Captain she wouldn't be jumping again. And that was that.

Four days into World War One, Dolly and her sister, Wene, joined the Women's Emergency Corps, which became the Women's Volunteer Reserve. The summer of 1915 saw Dolly driving munitions in a two-ton truck for the War Department. Her most memorable load was two tons of camouflaged gold bullion, which she carried alone across London; she was quite unaware of what had been on board.

In 1917 Dolly joined the newly-formed Women's Auxiliary Corps and volunteered for service oversees as a driver-mechanic, driving officers on the Western Front in France. The work was frequently dangerous and on one occasion she carried a live shell in

*Shortly before her death Dolly was the guest of the RAF Falcons Parachute Display Team at Eastbourne Air Show, in July 1983*

the boot of her car until it was detonated.

Her worst experience was getting frostbite, when the surgeon replaced two of her toes on each foot with those from the amputated foot of a wounded soldier. When the 'flu epidemic of 1918 raged through the lines and the hospital, Dolly's sick bed was wheeled into the kitchen, from where she organised the feeding of the entire hospital for several days.

Among the VIPs she drove – the American General Thompson, President Poincaré of France and King Albert I of Belgium – was Captain Sedgwick, the rent and lands officer, who, she learned, objected vehemently to women drivers. It was a strange beginning to a relationship with the man she later married. They set up home on the outskirts of Blackheath and had one child, Molly.

In the 1930s Dolly became involved in voluntary welfare work with schools. At the start of the Second World War she helped evacuate children and pregnant mothers from London to the country, then she joined the Auxiliary Fire Service as a volunteer part-time driver. Dolly was later involved in air-raid shelter work, finally taking the senior post of Shelter Staff Officer for Lewisham.

After the war the family moved to Bonchurch on the Isle of Wight, where they lived for the next seventeen years. Dolly's husband died in 1956, and in 1962 Dolly and Molly moved to Eastbourne, where Dolly entered into the life of the town, and did trolley service at an old people's home until she was eighty-six, despite suffering from an arthritic hip.

Perhaps her greatest joy was to renew her contacts with the world of parachutists. She met the Red Devils and was fascinated by their parachute harnesses and 'free fall'. At the age of ninety she flew with the Red Devils when they gave a display over Worthing. In the aeronautical world, she was always Dolly Shepherd, whereas to all but a very few she was Elizabeth Sedgwick. It was only just before her death that it was known she was one and the same person.

Dolly died in September 1983, and both the Red Devils and the RAF Falcons were represented at her funeral. In his tribute, the Reverend Edward Tennick praised her courage, spirit and endurance, her zest for life and an equal zest for the welfare of others – and a heart filled with love and compassion. The *Eastbourne Herald* referred to Dolly as 'one of the most intrepid, charming and colourful characters ever to have lived in Eastbourne'.

Dolly's story lives on in the pages of her book, *When the 'Chute Went Up,* and in the illustrated talks given by her daughter, Molly. Dolly appears in many aeronautical and aviation books, is on one of the murals at the Alexandra Palace, and her exploits are on display at several museums. Her story has been aired on both radio and television.

# 'A Writer is not One Who Can but One Who *Does*'

## E F BENSON (1867-1940)

A writer is one who does! There must be few writers who were able to fulfil their own maxim so well as EF Benson. Benson, always known as Fred, produced almost 100 books – novels, biographies, plays, articles and other non-fiction flowed from his fluent pen like water rushing down a stream. And among them were several masterpieces still read to this day.

Fred's father, Edward White Benson, as a handsome young clergyman of twenty-four, had proposed to his pretty twelve-year-

*Benson at nineteen*

old cousin, Mary (Minnie) Sidgwick. And from then until she turned eighteen, Minnie did her best to improve herself to be worthy of this upwardly mobile churchman, who later became Archbishop of Canterbury. They married when Edward was headmaster of Wellington College. Minnie was determined to be a good wife but, sadly, realised that she was not in love with Edward as she thought she ought to be, and their Paris honeymoon was a disaster.

Despite these problems, during the early years of her marriage Minnie was kept busy with successive child-bearing. Martin was born in 1860, Arthur in 1862, Maggie in 1865, Edward Frederick in 1867 and Hugh in 1871. In 1872, when her husband accepted the post of Chancellor of Lincoln Cathedral, Minnie suffered a nervous breakdown. She found real happiness only after forming an inseparable friendship with Lucy Tait, daughter of the former Archbishop of Canterbury.

But to return to the life of Fred. After the Easter holiday of 1876, when he was aproaching his eleventh birthday, Fred was sent to Temple Grove preparatory school at East Sheen, near Richmond. As an author-to-be, he found a wonderfully varied mix of teachers, from the headmaster downwards, on whom to work his imagination. He later recalled: 'I cannot believe a stranger set of instructors were ever got together'.

On September 17, 1881, Edward delivered Fred personally to Marlborough, where the boys were much impressed by the bishop's clerical garb. Fred spent the happiest days of his life at Marlborough and even picked up a scholarship available to sons of clergymen.

Edward again took Fred to his next step up the scholastic ladder – to King's College, Cambridge – on October 4, 1887. The undergraduate took easily to the life there, as he had at Marlborough. In those days, Cambridge provided a bizarre, privileged, archaic atmosphere, where young men were encouraged to do very little with the greatest style and *elan*.

At the end of 1887 Fred won an exhibition at King's, which took away the financial burden and, most importantly for the budding writer, allowed him to write whatever he chose. With the co-operation of a friend, he started the *Cambridge Fortnightly,* which lasted only five issues. When the magazine folded, Fred turned his attention to publishing his first book, extracts of which appeared in his old school magazine, *The Marlburian.*

After gaining a first class honours degree, Fred was persuaded by his father to spend an extra year at Cambridge, when he studied archaeology and again passed with honours in 1891. Armed with this academic achievement, he worked in Athens for the British School of Archaeology, and in Egypt for the Society for the Promotion of Hellenic Studies.

He was considering the possibility of earning his living as an author. No doubt he was spurred on by the modest success of his brother, Arthur, already a published author, and now remembered chiefly for writing the words of Land of Hope and Glory, to fit Elgar's Pomp and Circumstance No 1. Fred sent a short story to *Blackwood's Magazine* and, like many young writers, he suffered rejection.

But he was also working on a novel, which ultimately became one of his greatest successes. He sent the manuscript to Methuen, who immediately accepted it. The book was to change the life of EF Benson for ever. For of all the many books he would subsequently write throughout his career, there would be few ever to attain the success of *Dodo*. The first edition sold out within a month and ran to twelve editions in under a year. Fred was abroad in Athens at the time of publication and returned to find himself a celebrity and his book a sensational best-seller.

Today's readers find the central character, Dodo, highly unrealistic, and her conversation improbable. But in 1894 this was exactly how high society women behaved and talked. Benson never married and his protrayal of women in fiction often showed a cruel streak. It caused several critics to reason that he disliked women.

Fred was still officially an archaeologist and made several more trips to Greece and Egypt. Among his friends at the time was the poet, Lord Alfred Douglas, currently embroiled in his disastrous affair with Oscar Wilde. Douglas spent a week at Fred's lodgings in Athens.

Returning home from one of his Greek visits, Fred discovered an as-yet-to-be-ruined Capri and found it enchanting. There he encountered a number of other single men, all of whom were enjoying the privilege of being left alone. On Fred's return home, his father was anxious for him to become an education officer, but Fred said that he had quite made up his mind to be a writer, something of which his father disapproved.

His next publication was a collection of short stories called *Six Common Things*. It was not well received, and his next three books were savagely torn to pieces by the critics.

Fred's father died, in church, on Sunday, October 16, 1896. The family moved out of Lambeth Palace and bought a house in Winchester for £4,000. Despite his preference to live alone, Fred moved into the new house as he had promised his father he would. The rest of the household consisted of Minnie, and Fred's three sisters, Lucy, Maggie and Beth.

Fred was not at all keen on Winchester although it was full of the people whom he enjoyed most – the titled and the amusing – and entertained whenever he could. This did not, however, please the rest of the family and Minnie had to ask him, in the name of economy, to stop inviting people to stay. In the spring of 1898 he returned to Greece where he gave assistance to Greek refugees from the Turks, and sent reports to *The Times*.

The family decided to move further into the country and leased a seventeenth century manor house, Tremans, near Horsted Keynes in Sussex. Fred, now thirty-two, rented a bachelor flat in Oxford Street, London and regularly dined out, went to theatres, concerts and art galleries, and enjoyed all the pleasures the capital had to offer. He even acquired a gentleman's gentleman, of which his mother strongly disapproved.

Minnie complained of his idleness. For to her, just being a writer signalled a life of doing nothing. But as well as being the darling of society, Fred did get down to some serious writing. It was no chore. Words poured effortlessly from his pen. He even launched *The Imperial and Colonial Review* from his flat. The magazine had only a limited life as Fred neglected distribution and gave it no publicity.

He had more success with his next books, *Mannon and Co* (1899), in which he returned to the theme of society, and *Princess Sophia* (1900). The proceeds were sufficiently profitable to enable Fred to employ two maids, retain his man servant and run two residences – his flat in Oxford Street and a house at 3 St Cross Street. He wrote two more books and a play for the actress Mrs Patrick Campbell. This, unfortunately, opened in New York to a very frosty reception.

There followed two stories for *The Onlooker* and, in 1901, his best professional success since *Dodo*. This was *The Luck of the Veils*, part satire, part horror story.

It has long been an open question whether Fred was homosexual. Certainly he enjoyed the company of attractive young men. And as he grew older he tried to spend at least some time every summer on Capri. The island openly attracted homosexual men and Italian law had permitted sexual relations between men as early as 1891. The young men on the island behaved naturally, free of inhibition. Fred led the life of a hedonist, swimming, sunbathing, drinking wine and gossiping. In one of his later books,

*Colin,* he dealt with the sensual pleasure experienced by his young hero, Nino, whose 'black hair grew on his forehead, the black lashes swept by his smooth brown cheek'. In one of the poems Fred wrote to a friend in Venice, he described local youths as: 'Nude white pillars of manhood beneath the night'.

At the age of only forty-five Fred's good health began to deteriorate. He suffered excruciating pain in one of his kidneys and in 1913 the diseased kidney was removed.

Fred was too old to enlist at the outbreak of World War One, but like other well-known writers he was summoned to Whitehall to write propaganda for the war effort. The nature of the work prompted Fred to act mysteriously, as if he were withholding top secret information that he could not divulge. At the end of the war he was awarded the MBE for his work, which had included running a charity for the wounded in hospitals and convalescent homes.

In 1913 Fred had found a beautiful new home at 25 Brompton Square, Knightsbridge, which was to be his London address for the rest of his life. So inspired was he with his new home that he produced three books in the first year there. Of these, *David Blaize* was an immediate critical success. Obviously based on Fred's own school days, it deals frankly with romantic affection between two adolescent boys. Gone is the prattle betwen robots, as seen in his early novels.

Shortly afterwards Fred's brother, Arthur, was committed temporarily to an Ascot nursing home for the insane, and their mother died in 1918, aged seventy-six. During this period Fred's most successful book, *Queen Lucia,* was published, and then the first of many autibiographical works, *Our Family Affairs* (1920) and *Mother* (1925).

Henry James, the Benson family friend, had for many years occupied Lamb House in the historic Sussex town of Rye. Fred visited James there in 1900 and continued to call on the American writer whenever he had the chance. James would spend hours in the Garden Room, an extension that jutted out at right-angles to the main house, dictating to his secretary. After James died in 1916, and after several other people took on the lease of Lamb House, it came eventually to Fred. With Arthur, still in frail health, he took a joint lease of Lamb House and some of the brothers' best work was produced there.

Fred's next significant title, *Miss Mapp,* was set in Rye, Benson's fictional Tilling. Readers felt an envious kind of contempt for his chief character and Fred refers in the novel to 'her malignant curiosity and her cancerous supicions about all her friends' and the 'acidities', which well up in her fruitful mind. But it is a tribute to Fred's skill that he was able to make her hilariously funny. He laughed at his character's absurdities but also forgave them.

*Benson, from a drawing by Frank Slater, 1926*

Fred knew real women similar to Miss Mapp and told Compton Mackenzie that he had met some extraordinary women in Rye 'fussy and eager and alert and preposterous'.

Fred was called mean in some quarters, notably by the infamous lesbian couple, Radclyff Hall and Una Troubridge, both residents of Rye. They disapproved of him for being so buttoned-up. Fred, on the other hand, considered open lesbianism vulgar.

After Arthur's death in 1925 Fred published three books in three years, the most important of which was *Phairsees and Publicans,* which came out in 1926. It contained the theme common in many of Fred's books – that goodness resides in self-sacrifice. This is an intense, personal book that reveals Fred's true opinion of the silly creatures of his fiction – the Mapps and Lucias, all set in Rye.

Two biographies followed, *Sir Francis Drake* and *The Life of Alcibiades.* The latter was much praised as scholarly and disciplined, calling upon Fred's wide knowledge of classical literature. Then, for light relief, this was followed by *Paying Guests,* about a batch of dotty English characters.

Then came what has been called Fred's masterpiece – *As We Were*. It is an account of the kind of high society that disappeared during the First World War. Fred's stature as a writer now earned him accolades from the town of Rye. He was made a magistrate, and when Queen Mary visited the town in 1935, he was chosen to escort her around the antique shops.

At home at Lamb House, the place was well run with a staff of three indoors plus a gardener. Fred took a great interest, both in what was planted, and what was on the menu for every meal. The cellar was well stocked with good wine and home-made barley water for the hot days of summer.

A typical writer's day started with a cold bath, run by his manservant, Charlie. Breakfast was at nine, followed by a read of the papers. Fred stuck to a schedule of 2,000 words a day. For the writer, he believed, was someone who *does* write, not someone who can. Books kept rolling off the EF Benson production line. There was a volume of *Spook Stories,* a fourth Lucia adventure, *Lucia's Progress,* and a biography, *Queen Victoria.*

In 1933, following his success as a mgaistrate, he was invited by the town council to become Rye's mayor. He accepted and was invested as the 645th Mayor of Rye in 1934, splendidly arrayed in medieval costume. Faithful to tradition, he threw pennies from the balcony of the George Hotel, to be gathered by a scrabble of eager children on the ground below. During his three-year mayoralty he was forced to supplement his meagre salary from personal funds. However, the office took him to some great events – the Jubilee of George V, the succession and abdication of Edward VIII and the coronation of George VI. In 1935 Fred became Speaker of the Cinque Ports in another quaint ceremony.

But death was already waiting in the wings. After smoking between twenty and thirty cigarettes every day during his adult life, he suddenly began to lose weight and cough relentlessly. Fred had once written about death in one of his plays: 'To the weary I am rest, to the sad I am consolation. To those who mourn I am comfort, to the happy I am the consummation of their happiness.'

He had a medical examination at University College Hospital at the beginning of 1940 and was found to have terminal cancer of the throat. He died on February 29, glad to know that his last book, *Final Edition,* was going to press. This and his other hundred or so books would act as his epitaph.

✳ ✳ ✳

# Mr Brighton –
# The Champagne Socialist

## LEWIS COLEMAN COHEN (1897-1966)

This human dynamo dominated Brighton politics for more than thirty years, so much so that he was referred to as Mr Brighton. He made one fortune, lost it then built up another, even richer and more successful. As his life demonstrated, Lewis Cohen was a capitalist in his work but a socialist in his sympathies. And, despite being a thorn in the flesh of the permanent local Tory majority, he succeeded in being the town's most popular and imaginative mayor. Houses and housing were his constant interest and he single-handedly founded the Alliance Building Society.

Lewis Coleman Cohen was born on March 28, 1897, at 17 Priory Avenue, Hastings. The family had a jewellery shop at 26 White Rock and were prominent members of the town's small Jewish community. There were two other boys in the family, Maurice, and Reggie the youngest. Lewis was a natural leader and both boys looked to their elder brother for guidance. Lewis was accepted by Hastings Grammar School, where he stayed until the age of eleven; he also spent some time in Brussels to learn French.

Around the turn of the nineteenth century, the family had got into financial difficulties and when, in 1910, Hyam, the boys' father, died from diabetes, there was very little money left. Their mother, Esther, and the boys moved to the basement of 22 York Road in Brighton, a boarding house owned by Hyam's sisters. Lewis and his brothers were accepted by Brighton, Hove and Sussex Grammar School. But money was desperately short and at the age of thirteen and a half, Lewis had to go out to work.

He was employed by Reason and Tickle, estate agents, for just five shillings a week. He was promised a wage of £1 a week after three years, but was given only 17s 6d, and this prompted him to apply for a job with the rival agents, Graves, Son and Pilcher. Here he earned £1 a week plus commission. Regularly he put a part of his earnings aside and, by the age of twenty-three, he had saved the then substantial sum of £400. It was enough to buy out Reason and Tickle.

Part of what drove him were the memories of his youth. He would never forget the poverty of Brighton's poorest citizens, from whom it was his job to collect rents. From these experiences he made a lifetime commitment to socialist ideals, despite the fact that many other members of the Cohen family were staunch Tories. At the age of seventeen Lewis joined the Labour Party and later helped set up its first branch in Brighton.

At the outbreak of the First World War Lewis was a peace-time officer cadet with the Royal Field Artillery, where his medical record was overlooked. He had had tuberculosis when he was twelve and this now disqualified him from joining the armed services. Nevertheless, the carnage of the war, even at a distance, made him a commited pacifist.

His socialist beliefs were well tested by the general strike of May 1926. A rock was thrown through the windscreen of his car and, during a noisy demonstration, he escaped from being clubbed by police only by climbing over a wall. His sympathy with the strikers also affected his thriving estate agency as his biggest client took away his rent collecting business.

But despite these setbacks Lewis's agency thrived. He was also a keen gadgets man and several of his ideas enjoyed a measure of success. One was a prototype of the automatic photo booth and this netted him £11,000. However, he then lost the lot on another scheme – a device for closing doors quietly. Still another failure was the founding of the Duchess Theatre in London, which had to be sold at a huge loss.

Lewis was nevertheless anxious to expand his agency and he set his eyes on a number of sleepy building societies. One by one he acquired them, the biggest catch of all being the Manchester and Salford Permanent Building Society, with assets of more than half a million pounds. Lewis changed the rules by which societies had operated. He asked for smaller deposits from house-buyers and allowed longer periods during which they could pay off the loan. Lewis's new building society, the amalgamation of several smaller societies, was called the Brighton and Sussex Building Society (BSBS).

During the 1920s and 1930s there was an unprecedented growth in house building and house ownership. Lewis's terms for a £399 freehold were, typically, £25 down and 11s 3d weekly repayments. Other building societies called Lewis's methods brash, vulgar and overly modern, but in time all others would follow his lead.

It was during the 1930s that Lewis began a lifelong struggle to enter parliament. He was to try many times and never succeed. Brighton was too staunchly Tory. But in 1930 he won a council seat, which he held for a year, and he was appointed chairman of Brighton Labour Party.

Lewis seemed to acquire girl friends easily – though to his male friends he was rather plain looking. But women seemed to find something else. Perhaps it was his vitality, maybe his success. He had many short-lived romances but, towards the end of the 1930s, when he was in his early forties, he yearned for a longer, more lasting relationship. In 1938, at a Fabian summer school, he met just the right person. She was the beautiful, strong-willed and high-minded Sonya Lawson, aged twenty-four. She was the youngest daughter of a Jewish family with a clothes shop in Finsbury, London.

With the Second World War barely months away, Sonya, anxious to escape, set sail for South Africa. Lewis bombarded her with letters and cables to the ship asking her to return and marry him. For fear of hostilities, rather than Lewis's pleading, the ship turned back to England. Lewis and Sonya were married at Hove register office on September 23, and spent their honeymoon cycling around Sussex on a tandem.

At forty-three, Lewis was too old to be conscripted into the armed servies, and would anyway, have failed his medical because of the tuberculosis of his youth. He joined the Home Guard and spent the early part of the war patrolling the South Downs. Invasion was feared to be imminent and the southern coast was barricaded with barbed wire.

Lewis and Sonya bought a fine house, Lattenbells, in Farm Lane, Ditchling, and converted the cellar into an air-raid shelter. Sonya was briefly evacuated to Sidmouth in Devon and their son, John, was born there on July 13, 1940. But by the time their second child, Christine, was born on May 6, 1942, Sonya was back in Brighton.

At the outbreak of war the BSBS had assets of £4 million, with prime sites all over the country. But rapidly dwindling house prices, and a run on withdrawals, slashed assets by more than £500,000. Lewis met the crisis head-on by changing the society's name to the Alliance and organising the business to be run on a national basis.

Meanwhile, his marriage was often at breaking point. Lewis wanted a traditional Jewish wife, which Sonya resisted. She was strong-willed, independent and a feminist. Neither partner was ready to compromise.

On July 11, 1946, Madeleine, their third child, was born. Sonya wanted to live apart for a while and took the children to California. Lewis persuaded her to return, but a growing family and the privations of post-war austerity only highlighted their differences. They remained together for another nine months, when Sonya and the children left for South Africa. This time there was to be no reconciliation and the couple divorced in 1951.

After the war, in 1945, Lewis again tried to enter parliament but failed. In 1951 he tried again and by this time he was leader of the local Labour Party. He campaigned hard but lost to his Conservative rival, Howard Johnson. In later years, Johnson admitted that the best man lost.

During the 1950s, the Alliance grew rapidly. In the mortgage business Lewis continued to fight for longer periods of repayments and no-deposit/100 per cent mortgages. He also helped change the thinking in raising mortgages on flats. He rightly foresaw the time when banks would loan money on homes.

In 1958, for the first time, the Alliance's half-yearly interest payments to shareholders and depositers was more than £1 million. Lewis saw this as a time for celebration and organised a luncheon at the Royal Pavilion. Howard Johnson, Lewis's past political opponent, was now an Alliance director. He freely admitted that the Alliance's enormous success was the result of the efforts of one man. 'Lewis,' he said, 'was a first class financial adviser. He knew the money markets, and had a great knowledge of big city finance houses.'

Lewes was a generous employer, but a tough one. There was a proper restaurant for the staff ('not a plastic tablecloth canteen'), free morning coffee and afternoon tea, games rooms and a superbly-equipped sports ground. And of course – being a building society – employees could also buy their own homes on very advantageous terms.

However, a common complaint was that he made no distinction between work time and leisure hours. His secretaries were always in tears, always leaving and always coming back. His directors were quite used to Lewis making demands on them at any time of the day or night.

But despite his unbridled work ethic, Lewis never forgot his family. He was concerned about his children's education and in 1953 her persuaded Sonya to return from Cape Town with the children. They moved back into their old house in Ditchling and Lewis accepted the fact that he and Sonya would never again come together. But happily, they remained friends. Lewis adored his chidren and called regularly at the house.

At the same time, Lewis could never stray far from

*Lewis Cohen, the mayor on a bicycle*

politics and he now set his cap at becoming Brighton's mayor. But to gain the support of the Tory majority on the council, Lewis was forced to make a pledge that he would never again fight a parliamentary election.

The Tories were as good as their word and Lewis was elected mayor in 1956. He was determined to make his mayoralty the most outstanding Brighton had ever seen. He started with a record-breaking banquet and instead of the traditional Royal Pavilion, he hired the larger Corn Exchange for more than 470 guests. Food, decorations, and the four-hour dinner were imaginative and lavish.

He cabled greetings around the world to forty-five other towns called Brighton.

Other celebrations followed. At his own expense, he invited the 160-strong Soviet Red Army Choir and treated them to lunch at the Royal Pavilion. There was a fancy dress ball for children and teas for old age pensioners.

Lewis was known for his eccentricity, and when the High Commissioner for New Zealand invited him to an informal picnic, he took the invitation literally and turned up in cycling shorts on a battered old bike. His host took some convincing that this really was the mayor of Brighton. Lewis would be rememberd as the mayor who rocked 'n' rolled at his ball, the one who stripped off to swim at a children's gala – and of course the mayor on the bicycle.

Throughout his business life, Lewis had played a straight bat – tough but honourable. Everyone knew his word could be trusted. So why did he now so shamelessly break his word? After accepting Conservative terms for his mayoral election – that he would never again stand for parliament – this is exactly what he did. He put his name forward for the constituency of Kemp Town.

The *Evening Argus* of April 6, 1957, made an attempt to defend him. The paper cited blatant Tory opposition to Lewis while he was mayor. But this excuse was meaningless. The Tories had made no pledge that they would agree with everything the mayor said. Did Lewis believe they did? Perhaps this was the case. For Lewis admitted that Tory opposition made him feel he had a freer hand.

At times, this overriding desire to be an MP seemed to block out everything else. Lewis had friends in the hierarchy of the Labour Party and he had reason to believe that if he were elected, he would be involved in the housing policy of the party – and this had always been his passion. It was all a huge temptation.

But there were other priorities in his sprawling business empire. A new building was needed for the expanding company, and a head office was built next to Hove Park at a cost of just under half a million pounds.

In 1960, at a dinner party in London, Lewis met the woman with whom he would share the happiest years of his life. This was Renie Bodlender, the forty-five-year-old widow of a Yorkshire businessman. She was warm, attractive, intelligent and vibrant with two grown-up children. For Lewis, it was love at first sight and as he got to know her better, he found they shared a number of interests. Among their favourites were the theatre, parties, and golf, and they were soon inseparable. In November 1961, they married at a small, private ceremony at the Brighton and Hove Liberal Synagogue. They spent their honeymoon in South Africa.

The staff of the Alliance were stuck for an appropriate present for their chairman who had everything. Unaware that his first marriage had started on a tandem, this is exactly what they now bought him. Decorated with L-plates, it was described as 'the perfect gift for a cycling tycoon'.

Lewis has been described as Brighton's one-man benevolent fund. He seemed incapable of saying no, and people came to him in their thousands. He found homes for refugees, supported innumerable charities (especially Jewish ones) and bent over backwards to give mortgages to virtually everyone who asked. He gave freely to the Labour Party, paid for ward parties, and bought the Kemp Town headquarters.

For several years there had been rumours that Lewis would be offered a peerage. It was generally thought that it was richly deserved. But it wasn't until April 1965, during a council meeting, that he was summoned to the telephone to take a call from the Prime Minister. Harold Wilson offered to make him Lord Cohen of Brighton, and Lewis gladly accepted. A few weeks later, Wilson rang Lewis to ask when he planned to take up his seat in the Lords. Lewis estimated he would be ready in about three months and began giving his reasons for the delay. The Prime Minister cut in to say Lewis was needed to lead for the government in the housing debate the following week. Lord Cohen had finally arrived in Westminster.

But Lewis was slowing down, his body reacting to the constant demands made on it. On October 21, 1966, after a long illness, he died of leukaemia. The Brighton and Hove New Synagogue in Holland Road, Hove, wasn't nearly big enough for the crowd that turned up for his funeral. A week later, on Thursday November 3, there was an even larger memorial service in the Brighton Dome, to which the great and the good came in reverence. The Prime Minister, Harold Wilson, sent this tribute.

'His whole life was a search for the right answers to the relevant questions. That he is now so widely mourned, is a tribute to his principles and to his courage.'

✳ ✳ ✳

# BIBLIOGRAPHY

Adlard, John, *Stenbock, Yeats, and the Nineties,* Cecil & Amelia Woolf, 1969

Benson, EF, *As We Were,* Hogarth Press, 1985

Benson, EF, *Final Edition,* Longmans Green

Briffett, David, *The Acid Bath Murders,* Field Place Press, 1988

Candlin, L, *Tales of Old Sussex,* Countryside Books, 1985.

Copper, Bob, *A Song for Every Season,* Coppersongs, 1997

Copper, Bob, *Early to Rise,* Heinemann, 1976

Dickson, Lovat, *Half-Breed, the Story of Grey Owl,* Peter Davies, 1939

Dickson, Lovat, *Wilderness Man, the Strange Story of Grey Owl,* Macmillan, 1973

Fisher, Michael H, *The First Indian Author in English, Dean Mahomed,* Oxford University Press, 1996

Green, Andrew, *Ghost Hunting, a Practical Guide,* Garstone Press, 1973

Hutchinson, Geoff, *Fuller of Sussex, a Georgian Squire,* published by the author, 1997

Hyman, Alan, *The Rise and Fall of Horatio Bottomley,* Cassell, 1972

Knox, Rawle, ed, *The Work of EH Shepard,* Methuen Children's Books 1979

La Bern, Arthur, *Haigh, the Mind of a Murderer,* WH Allen, 1973

Lefebure, Molly, *Murder with a Difference,* Heinemann, 1958

Masters, Brian, *The Life of EF Benson,* Chatto & Windus, 1991

Millar, Ronald, *The Piltdown Mystery,* SB Publications, 1998

Palmer, Geoffrey, and Lloyd, Noel, *EF Benson As He Was,* Lennard Publishing, 1988

Scutt, RWB, and Christopher Gotch, *Art, Sex, and Symbol,* Cornwall Books of America, 1986

Shepard, EH, *Drawn from Memory,* Methuen, 1957

Shepard, EH, *Drawn from Life,* Methuen, 1961

Shepherd, Dolly, with Peter Hearn & Molly Sedgwick, *When the 'Chute Went Up, Adventures of a Pioneer Lady Parachutist,* Robert Hale, 1984, Revised edition, Skyline, 1996

Spencer, Frank, *Piltdown - a Scientific Forgery,* British Museum, 1990.

Symons, Julian, *Horatio Bottomley,* The Cresset Press, 1955

Thwaite, Ann, *AA Milne, His Life,* Faber and Faber, 1990

Vaisey, David, ed, *The Diary of Thomas Turner,* 1754-1765, Oxford University Press, 1984

Walsh, John Evangelist, *Unravelling Piltdown,* Random House, 1998

Weiner, Joseph, *Solution of the Piltdown Problem,* British Museum, 1953

Worster, Dean K, *The Life and Times of Thomas Turner of East Hoathly,* Yale University Press, 1948

*Sussex County Magazine,* various

# INDEX

Copper, Bob, 12-17; first job as tar-boy, 13; joins police, 13; runs Central Social Club, Peacehaven, 13; BBC broadcast from Eight Bells pub,1950, 13-14; *A Song From Every Season* published 1971, awarded Best Book of the Year, 14; more books published, 16

Copper, James (Brasser, Bob's grandfather) 12, 15; born 1845, 12; made farm bailiff, 12; 'half a hundred' songs noted by a Mrs Kate Lee in 1898, 15

Copper, Jim (Bob's father, James' son) broadcast from Eight Bells pub, 1950, 13-14, made farm bailiff, 13; death, 15

Dawson, Charles (one of Piltdown men) 52-56

Dickson, Lovat (Grey Owl's publisher) 35

Doyle, Sir Arthur Conan (one of Piltdown men) 54-55

Durand-Deacon, Olive (one of John Haigh's victims) 40-41

Ealing Society for the Investigation of Psychic Phenomena, 28

English Folk Dance and Song Society, 14

Fuller, John (Mad Jack) 18-22; at Eton, 18; ancestors, 18; proposed marriage, 18; sex life, 18; at House of Commons, 19-20; follies, 20-22; founder of Royal Institution, 22

George, Prince of Wales, 42, 45

Gladys (wife of the Great Omi) 49-50

Grant, Pauline, 23-26; at St Clare's, 24; at Bolney, 24; number of animals in her care, 26

The Great Omi, 47-51; army service, 47, 49; illus, 48; entertaining the troops, 51; death, 51

Green, Andrew, 27-31; ghosts are...28; ghostly experiences, 29-30; equipment for ghost-hunting, 31; illus, 29

Grey Owl, see Belaney, Archie

Haigh, John George, 37-41; drinks victims' blood, 37, 41; early years, 37; illus, 38; marriage, 38; first murder, 39; workshop in London, 38-39; workshop in Crawley, 40; confession, 41

Hailsham, 51

Hemstead Farm, Uckfield, 25

Hendersons, Dr Archie and wife (two of John Haigh's victims) 40